WITHDRAWN

HARTFORD PUBLIC LIBRARY
Alexandria, Ohio

Who Are the Handicapped?

Other books by the author

DIARY OF A HARLEM SCHOOLTEACHER
RESISTANCE: PROFILES IN NONVIOLENCE
THE WAR AND THE PROTEST: VIETNAM
REVOLUTIONARIES: AGENTS OF CHANGE
PROFILES IN BLACK POWER
RELIGIONS
BLACK MANIFESTO FOR EDUCATION, editor
A PIECE OF THE POWER: FOUR BLACK MAYORS
FROM LEW ALCINDOR TO KAREEM ABDUL JABBAR
THE PSYCHOLOGY OF BLACK LANGUAGE
  (with Hugh F. Butts, M.D.)
JOKES FROM BLACK FOLKS
PINCKNEY BENTON STEWART PINCHBACK
RALPH BUNCHE: A MOST RELUCTANT HERO
ADAM CLAYTON POWELL: PORTRAIT OF A
  MARCHING BLACK
STREET GANGS: YESTERDAY AND TODAY
WITCHCRAFT, MYSTICISM AND MAGIC IN THE
  BLACK WORLD
JOBS IN BUSINESS AND OFFICE
BABE RUTH AND HANK AARON: THE HOME RUN
  KINGS
SNOW SCULPTURE AND ICE CARVING
THE CREOLES OF COLOR OF NEW ORLEANS
FIGHTING SHIRLEY CHISHOLM
THE CONSUMER MOVEMENT
THE PICTURE LIFE OF MALCOLM X
DR. J: A BIOGRAPHY OF JULIUS ERVING
YOUR RIGHTS: PAST AND PRESENT
THE STORY OF STEVIE WONDER
ALWAYS MOVIN' ON: A BIOGRAPHY
  OF LANGSTON HUGHES
A NEW KIND OF JOY: THE STORY OF THE SPECIAL
  OLYMPICS
THE LONG STRUGGLE: AMERICAN LABOR
TEENAGE ALCOHOLISM
PELÉ: A BIOGRAPHY
THE LIFE AND DEATH OF MARTIN LUTHER
  KING, JR.

Who Are the Handicapped?

JAMES HASKINS

DOUBLEDAY & COMPANY, INC.
GARDEN CITY, NEW YORK

ISBN 0-385-09609-7 Trade
      0-385-09610-0 Prebound
Library of Congress Catalog Card Number 76–2777

Copyright © 1978 by James Haskins
All Rights Reserved
Printed in the United States of America
First Edition

Acknowledgments

I am grateful to the various institutions for the handicapped that supplied material and guidance on this book. Thanks are also due Mary Ellen Arrington, who typed the manuscript drafts, Kathy Benson, for her help, and especially to J. M. Stifle.

Preface

Prejudice is an irrational fear of or hatred for someone or something based on ignorance of that person or thing. When we think of prejudice, we tend to think in terms of racial, social, religious or sexual bias. In recent years the movements for black civil rights and equal rights for women have drawn attention to the plight of many victims of prejudice in this country.

There is, however, one very substantial group of Americans, the victims of perhaps the cruelest kind of prejudice, who have remained largely unnoticed in the ongoing struggle for human pride and dignity—the more than 50 million Americans who suffer from some kind of physical or mental disability, who must bear the weight of the prejudice of the "normal." The prejudice against the disabled in our society has run so deep, for so long, it has become so ingrained in us, that it is almost an unconscious part of our lives. Most of us turn our heads away without thinking when we see someone who is deformed or disabled in some way.

Most of us, that is, except very young children. Although prejudice can become second nature, it must first be learned. Very young children will display a natural curiosity about those who are physically different from themselves, until they are taught to do otherwise. This curiosity is healthy, and if properly channeled and allowed to flourish, it will lead to an understanding of the causes and kinds of physical differences. On the other hand, learning to turn one's head only fosters the continuation of ignorance and prejudice. Instead of reprimanding children for their curiosity, we should encourage it. It is the adult who should learn from the child in this instance.

It is hoped that this volume will contribute to the elimination of prejudice against the disabled; that it will encourage all those who read it, young and old, to take a second look at those whose only social offense is a physical or mental difference over which they have no control; that it will promote a broader understanding of the disabled, particularly disabled children, in our society; and that it will draw attention to a varied and talented group of individuals with whom we have much more in common than we think.

Contents

Preface — vii

Part I: ATTITUDES
What Is Normal? — 3
Attitudes Toward the Disabled — 7
We Are All Handicapped — 17

Part II: BEING DISABLED
Who Are the Disabled? — 23
Being Blind — 25
Being Deaf — 39
Neurological Dysfunctions—Brain and Nerve Disorders — 51
- EPILEPSY — 52
- CEREBRAL PALSY — 57
- MULTIPLE SCLEROSIS — 62
- MUSCULAR DYSTROPHY — 66
- MENTAL RETARDATION — 67

Being Crippled — 75
A Word About Multihandicaps — 81

Part III: FUTURE OUTLOOK
What Next for the Disabled? — 85

Glossary — 97

Bibliography — 99

Index — 105

Part I

Attitudes

Let each become all that he was created capable of being; expand, if possible, to his full growth, and show himself at length in his own shape and stature, be these what they may.

THOMAS CARLYLE

What Is Normal?

According to the dictionary the word normal means, "conforming to a type or standard; regular . . . a common or natural condition . . . a usual or accepted rule or process." To be normal is to be typical, average, ordinary, commonplace. It is what is easily recognizable and readily understood.

We become accustomed to its reliability and feel secure in its soothing familiarity. We are willing to go to great lengths to protect that which is comfortingly normal, and we are fearful of anything that is "abnormal" or unusual—anything that we don't understand and fear may upset what we're used to. In order to bolster the foundations of normality against the threat, real or imagined, presented by what is unfamiliar, we equate normality with morality. To be normal is to be good, pure, true, right and, hence, praiseworthy. To be abnormal must therefore be the reverse—to be evil, unclean, false, wrong and worthy only of scorn.

In our society the normal tend to band together in an exclusive elite dedicated to the preservation of the status quo, and the pursuit of absolute normality. The physical ideal of the normal is embodied in the young, the beautiful, the graceful, the straight, the well-formed, the healthy. Homage is regularly paid to the ideal through a variety of social rituals and practices that include beauty contests, sports events, political elections, the award of celebrity status and media enshrinement. Those who do not measure up to the normal ideal are automatically suspect and, depending upon the degree of their deviation, are either tolerated, ignored or forcibly removed from society.

Of course, none of us can ever fully measure up to the ideal we have set for ourselves. An ideal is never meant to be completely attainable. It can never be real, but it is something we are all supposed to be striving to achieve.

Society is flexible, however, and allows for some degree of deviation from the norm. Just imagine what it would be like if we were all equally normal: We would all be exactly the same, like human dolls manufactured from a single mold. How boring! "Variety is the spice of life," and each of us represents a happy variation on the human norm.

Some of us have blue eyes, some brown, some hazel with flecks of gold; some have long silky hair, others have short and curly hair; some of us are tall, short, round or slim; some of us are fair, while others are dark, and still others are dotted with freckles. There are those of us who can sing like birds, while others have difficulty even carrying a tune; your handwriting might be clear and legible, while mine might look like "chicken scratchings." There are even some of us who have a crooked tooth or two, or a wart behind an ear, or a big toe that is separated from the others by a wide gap. Nobody finds it strange or odd that we have these variations. They are interesting. They're what makes each of us unique, and no one is shocked or amazed by them.

No one, that is, until these variations, these differences,

WHAT IS NORMAL?

take on a more obvious or dramatic form. Not until we see a man who has lost an arm, a girl with only two fingers on one hand, a boy in a wheel chair who can't control his bodily movements, a sightless woman with a long white cane making her way down the street, or a teen-ager who can't tie his shoes by himself do we react violently. These people become conspicuous because their differences are so apparent. They cannot hide them, so it is easy to single them out as abnormal.

It is when we, the normal, are confronted with such striking differences, that we become afraid. We call up all our centuries-old defenses against the intrusion of the grossly abnormal and move swiftly as an organized unit to expel the oddly disturbing element from our midst.

Why do we react this way toward physical deviance? What triggers this automatic defense mechanism? One observer feels that our fears regarding our own normality may make us uncomfortable with those who are different. Our fears regarding our own intactness may make us fear those who are not intact in some way. Insecurity about our own normality, along with ignorance about the causes and implications of physical deformity or disability, fear of the unknown, unfortunate myths about deviance that have become part of our cultural heritage, all contribute to our strongly negative reactions toward physical differences.

In order to overcome these negative reactions we must examine the origins of our irrational fears, dispel our ignorance and educate ourselves to the truth about physical disability. That is the purpose of this volume—to show the normal that the similarities between them and the disabled far outweigh the over-emphasized differences.

After all, what is the real difference between the person

with a gap between his toes and the one with a missing arm? One's difference is more noticeable than the other's, and it might possibly present more of a physical obstacle to be overcome than the other. That is all. The difference is only a matter of degree. The person with a serious disability is every bit as good, as beautiful, as human as the normal person, perhaps even more so, and that's what really counts.

One only need look at the accomplishments of some of the great men of history to realize this. Franklin Delano Roosevelt served as President of the United States for an unprecedented four terms that covered the period from the Great Depression through close to the end of the Second World War, while suffering the crippling effects of polio. Homer, the great poet of ancient Greece, author of the epic poems the *Illiad* and the *Odyssey*, was most likely blind. Napoleon, Emperor of France and one of the most brilliant military tacticians in history, is believed to have been epileptic. The musical genius Beethoven composed some of his greatest works after he had become completely deaf.

The accomplishments of these extraordinary men prove the axiom that it is what a person is inside—what he has to give—that is important, not how he might appear on the surface.

Attitudes Toward the Disabled

There is an ancient Greek legend of one Procrustes the innkeeper. Procrustes had only one size bed in all his inn—the "right" size—and all his guests were forced to sleep in the same sized bed no matter what their shape or form. The good innkeeper therefore found it necessary either to stretch his guests, who were too short for the bed, on the rack, in order that they might be the "right" size, or to saw off the feet of those who were too long, so that they too might fit his bed properly.

You may find this tale distasteful or outrageous, but it is not all that ridiculous when you consider the prevailing attitudes of the normal toward the deviant throughout history. The disabled or malformed person has traditionally been looked upon as a social misfit, and one who must be separated from society. This attitude was understandable in the earliest primitive cultures, where the profoundly disabled individual was a definite hindrance to the physical welfare of the whole group. The primitive tribe that depended upon hunting and gathering for sustenance could not afford to have a member who could not sustain himself; anyone who impeded the group's mobility, or could not do his share of the work necessary for survival, presented a threat to the lives of the rest and simply had to be abandoned for the sake of expediency.

As civilization progressed and societies became more stable and secure, attitudes toward physical disabilities did not change appreciably; only their justifications changed slightly. Although it was no longer absolutely necessary for the economic and physical survival of the group to exclude the handicapped, exclusion of them was considered expedient for religious and aesthetic reasons.

In ancient Greece, Sparta and Rome, where physical beauty and prowess were greatly valued and exalted, defective children were often put to death. Infants who did not live up to certain standards were left on mountainsides or thrown into rivers to die. Since the ancients had few medical explanations for the cause of such deviance, and since anything out of the ordinary was greatly feared, many superstitions and magico-religious explanations for deviance were adopted.

The physically disabled were alternately referred to as "demon-possessed," the "accursed of the gods," and at times even "protected of the gods," or "children of the gods." While most deviants were reviled and cast out, some, like the blind poet Homer and the prophet Phineas, were greatly revered. These contradictory attitudes of reverence and revulsion often existed side by side within the same society. Hebraic law, for example, admonished people to aid the unfortunate and disabled, while it simultaneously placed very stringent social and religious limitations on them. Leviticus 21:18–20 is quite specific about these limitations:

> 18. For whatsoever man he be that hath a blemish, he shall not approach: a blind man, or a lame, or he that hath a flat nose, or anything superfluous,

19. Or a man that is broken-footed, or broken-handed, or crookbacked, or a dwarf, or that hath a blemish in his eye, or is scurvy, or scabbed, or hath his bones broken;
20. no man . . . that hath blemish shall come nigh to offer the offerings of Jehovah made by fire: he hath a blemish; he shall not come nigh to offer the bread of God.

In short, no lame, maimed or otherwise physically deviant person was allowed to join the priesthood, offer sacrifices to God, or even enter the temple. (The Scriptures are equally stringent in their proscriptions regarding the physical nature of the sacrificial offering—no blemish is allowed there either.) The New Testament even recounts a story of Jesus Christ being condemned by the priests for healing a lame man in the temple on the Sabbath.

In the middle ages, an era that was not known for its humanitarianism, the disabled were often used for the amusement of the noble classes and were usually reduced to beggary among the lower. Jesters, Merry Andrews and other performers at court were commonly drawn from society's deviants—dwarfs, cripples, mental deficients—their bizarre appearance and behavior making them particularly amusing to their owners. Many from their ranks, however, became quite influential and gained positions of trust within the noble households. Some were known for their wit and cleverness and often became advisors and confidants of the master. Others have been immortalized in literature and song.

The era of the Protestant Reformation saw no reformation in society's attitudes toward physical disabilities. In fact, old superstitions were given new fire, and the belief that a twisted body automatically held a twisted soul gained firm hold upon the popular imagination. Martin Luther, the prime mover of the Reformation, declared that all cripples, cretins and other deviants were "changelings," i.e., demons in human form and, as such, unfit to live. He went so far as to declare that it would please God to see them destroyed.

The eighteenth century saw a slight shift in this attitude toward physical disabilities as the science of medicine began to flourish, and an interest was taken in the actual physiological causes and possible cures for disability. The nineteenth century saw a further softening of the purely clinical attitude of the previous century, as a more humanitarian and sentimental approach to the disabled was adopted. Although the prevailing feeling was gradually shifting from one of revulsion to one of pity, the disabled were still being separated from the rest of society, and housed in "asylums."

Today, even in so-called "enlightened" societies, our attitudes toward the disabled continue to reflect the legacy of fear, repugnance, superstition and myth we have inherited from our ancestors. Beliefs handed down for centuries aren't easily abandoned, no matter the weight of later scientific discoveries or the proofs of humanitarianism. There is still that lingering conviction that a disability is somehow the product of or punishment for wrong-doing. We still have the need to place blame somewhere, and charging deviance to the capriciousness of nature does not quite satisfy our craving.

Physical deviance is still shrouded in a cloak of shame and guilt that touches everyone who comes in contact with it, and, in our uneasiness, all we want is to remove the unsightly objects of our discomfort from our presence so that we can forget about them and the feelings they arouse.

The disabled have become an embarrassment to us—a reminder of our common guilt—so we must continue to put them away where we won't have to be made uncomfortable by their accusing presence. In order to assuage our consciences, we convince ourselves that what we are doing is for the best, anyway. After all, the poor creatures aren't fully human, they haven't the same power to reason and act that we do, so they're better off separated from the rest of us.

But what about the disabled? What about the feelings of the "poor creatures"? So far we have concerned ourselves only with the reactions and attitudes of the normal to the disabled, but what of their reaction to the normal world and to themselves? Are they objects fit only for pity or scorn? Are they less than human? The answer, of course, is an emphatic No. But after our enlightened society gets through with them they may very well become fit only for pity.

It should first of all be understood that a disabled person does not automatically perceive himself as abnormal or deviant. Like everyone else, he reasons and judges reality by what he experiences through his senses. If left alone, he would have no other standard with which to compare himself, outside of himself, and so he would quite naturally conclude that he was "normal." It is only when he comes in contact with society that he is made to realize that he is different, that he is somehow not quite like the others around him.

His assessment of that difference is based entirely on the reactions of those around him, for just like the rest of us, he sees himself in the mirror of other people's eyes. If the image he sees there is a negative one and he accepts what he sees, as most of us would, he will adopt a negative attitude toward his disability and himself. It is the normal world, therefore, that turns a disability into a handicap. Nature may cause a defect, but it is a hostile society that makes it a problem.

Society does this by magnifying the disability all out of proportion to its actual relation to the individual. It can't see the forest for the trees. It sees only the disability and so totally identifies the individual with his disability that he ceases to exist as anything but a disability. All other avenues for human development unaffected by that particular disability are automatically cut off, once that disability is recognized. The disabled person reads this in the eyes and attitudes of the normal world, and knows the bad news he sees is true because the normal world makes it true.

Obviously, this almost reflexive and predetermined reaction of the normal world toward the disabled has a profound effect on the personal development and self-perception of the disabled, especially those of the disabled child. Each child, as he grows, is expected to learn and adopt certain appropriate modes of behavior. For the disabled child there is added to these social expectations certain extra adjustments connected specifically with his deviation. Society's reaction to the child's disability, and its creation of a double standard for him place yet another and often debilitating strain on his personal growth.

To the disabled child, therefore, the normal world can appear uninviting and often quite hostile. It is a fearsome place fraught with obstacles and hidden dangers. It is a place where he is not really welcome; where he is at best pitied or ignored, and at worst actively oppressed, shoved aside, hidden away. Everywhere he turns he comes face to face with another impediment to his progress, and nowhere is our flagrant disregard for the disabled better represented than in the built-in barriers of our man-made environment.

Think of the child supported by braces and crutches confronted with a long flight of stairs, the person in a wheel chair sitting helplessly before a revolving door, or the sightless individual who cannot find a book he can read in the local library. These are but a few of the difficulties disabled people have to face every day of their lives because of what one doctor has called "the arrogance of the whole and healthy," who callously ignore the needs of the disabled when molding their environment.

This brings us right back to the legend of the Greek innkeeper who adjusted his guests to suit his bed size. Although we hope that today practices such as infanticide no longer exist in any but the most primitive societies where it might still be believed that a malformed infant is the work of the devil, the essential message of the normal to the disabled remains the same. If you can't adjust to the normal world, if you don't fit, then get out. Many of us still lock away defective children in darkened rooms, so they won't be seen by the neighbors. Within the last century or so institutionalization has become by far the most acceptable way of dealing with the disabled and the one we have convinced ourselves is the most humane, under the circumstances.

Since we have made it pretty well impossible for the disabled to function within our communities, we have created an alternate environment for them. When you think about it, this isolation, this warehousing of defective human beings, is really no more humane—quite possibly even less so—than the practice of leaving a deviant infant on a mountainside or throwing him in the river. The end result—the human waste—is the same. The process takes a little longer, although the damage to the human spirit is immediate.

The disabled person, who might otherwise have lived a full and productive life, is now routinely sentenced to live out his days in isolation, cut off from the support and acceptance of the community. Even if the disabled person manages to escape being condemned to an institution, his chances for a fulfilling life are slim. He is unlikely to receive education commensurate with his ability, to know the rewards of personal success, the warmth of social contact, or the satisfaction of a job well done. He will, in fact, even have trouble earning a living. For the most part, employers are afraid and unwilling to hire a disabled person because they don't think he can do the job. As one disabled person assesses the employment situation:

> In getting a job, there are a lot of people who don't want to hire the handicapped. People in general are afraid of something they don't know about. The average person doesn't know about the handicapped person whether he be blind, crippled or whatever, and there have been instances where an employer won't even accept an application, résumé or anything just because he knows you are blind . . .

It is little wonder that the disabled child, and later the adult, tends to withdraw and try to hide himself and his offensive defect from the unfriendly eyes of the normal world. At first he may try to deny his disability and pretend to be normal like everyone else, but that can't continue for long. He cannot escape from his disability, and we aren't about to let him escape from the fact that his presence is distasteful to us. Each day his disability be-

Franklin D. Roosevelt, the only man to be elected President of the United States four times, was afflicted with infantile paralysis (polio). He is seen here signing the Lend-Lease Bill in 1941. *(Franklin D. Roosevelt Library)*

Homer, the blind poet of Ancient Greece. *(Courtesy Museum of Fine Arts, Boston)*

Napoleon Bonaparte, one of the most brilliant military strategists in history, was believed to have suffered from epilepsy. *(Photographie Giraudon from le Musée Legion d'Honneur)*

Louis Braille developed a system of raised dots that allows blind people to read with their fingers. (*American Foundation for the Blind*)

Gilbert Ramirez, a justice of the Supreme Court of the State of New York, is blind. *(President's Committee on Employment of the Handicapped)*

Helen Keller, blind and deaf from infancy, overcame her severe disabilities and gained world renown for her accomplishments. *(American Federation for the Blind)*

Robert LaGrone, a successful computer programmer who works for International Business Machines, is blind. *(IBM Photo)*

The Honorable George C. Wallace, governor of Alabama and former candidate for the presidency. His hearing impairment did not hinder him in his political career. (*The Decatur, Alabama, Daily*)

comes ever more hateful to him, and in the end he is forced to accept the judgment of the normal world that he is ugly, insignificant, worthless. It finally becomes unavoidably clear that there is no place for him in the normal world.

We Are All Handicapped

> Fret not, my son. None of us is perfect. It is better to have crooked legs than a crooked spirit. We can only do the best we can with what we have. That, after all, is the measure of success! what we do with what we have.
>
> *The Door in the Wall*

History has painted a grim picture of the prospects for the disabled trying to function successfully in a normal world. But, fortunately, society's long-held attitudes of condescension, distaste and outright hostility in the face of physical deviation are slowly beginning to change. Gradually the disabled are being allowed out of the darkened closet and the institution into the light of day. And they are proving over and over again that when given the opportunity they can function quite satisfactorily in the normal world.

In spite of the apparent success of the many disabled who have been integrated into society, the normals are still reluctant to open the doors wide to all who clamor for full participation in their world. Centuries-old beliefs that a physical defect is somehow tainted with evil, or at the very least is unattractive or offensive, are not stamped out overnight. It takes time for people to be re-educated into thinking that a disabled person is in most ways just like the rest of us. We find it difficult, almost impossible to accept. We demand greater proofs.

What we are forgetting is that we are all of us disabled in some way. We all have some real or imagined problem or difficulty that presents an obstacle to self-fulfillment. Some of us aren't able to give easily; others don't know how to take graciously. Some are incapable of expressing their true feelings. Many of us find it difficult to speak in public or to defend ourselves against the attacks of others. There are those among us who are plagued by quick tempers. And there are many, many more of us who long to be something, someone, or somewhere else. All of these shortcomings, these personality defects or dissatisfactions, have their effect on the way we deal with the world. We know they limit us, but we don't let them dominate us. We don't let them prevent us from enjoying life as fully as we are able. We don't become our defects, we learn to overcome them and to get on with our lives.

It's no different for the physically disabled person. He knows he has a problem that limits him in certain ways. He also knows that he can function quite well within those limitations. He doesn't ask to be pitied or given special treatment, but most importantly, he does not want to be excluded on account of an accident of nature over which he has no control. All he wants is to be allowed the right to get on with his life, the same as anyone else. As one college professor, sightless from birth, expresses it for all the disabled:

> . . . if blindness hadn't been [the] obstacle, it could have been something else . . . Whether it's poverty, whether it's being a member of a minority group or some other reason—whatever it is—people are driven to do what they want or

need to do; and, qualitatively, being blind is no different than any of the other things . . .

Blindness means a lack of sight. It does not diminish a person's manhood or womanhood . . . the world belongs to us as much as it belongs to the sighted . . . We have the same rights to do and dare, succeed or fail, to be treated like human beings and to act like human beings as anybody else . . .*

The physically disabled are people, just like you and me. They have the same human needs for love, understanding and acceptance as the rest of us. They are just as capable of giving, taking, sharing and doing. All they ask is a fair chance to express their feelings and achieve their full potential as human beings.

*Edwin R. Lewinson. "Working in the Sighted World," recording, New York: American Foundation for the Blind, n.d.

Part II

Being Disabled

When we see people suffering or uncomfortable, we feel very sorry for them; but when we see them bravely bearing their sufferings, and making the best of their misfortunes, it is quite a different feeling. We respect, we admire them. One can respect and admire even a little child.

The Little Lame Prince

Who Are the Disabled?

In 1971 a National Center for Health Statistics survey estimated that about 51.1 million or one in four Americans suffers from a disability. Nearly two million Americans are legally blind. One in ten or 24 million Americans are limited in their mobility, and there are 250,000 victims of cerebral palsy in the United States alone. It is believed that 4 million people in this country suffer from epilepsy and that over 5,000 children are both deaf and blind. Another 6 million Americans are estimated to be mentally handicapped in varying degrees, with over 100,000 mentally retarded children being born each year.

What is the point of quoting all these statistics? The point is to show that it is no insignificant, ignorable, portion of our population that suffers from some form of limiting physical disability. It is to show that there are disabled persons in every state, in every county, in every community, and that no matter how hard we might try to avoid "the problem," we cannot. It touches all of us. You might have a grandfather who was a stroke victim and can't get around as well as he used to. Your aunt may have cataracts that impair her vision. Your best friend might have a brother who is deaf. You yourself might someday be crippled by accident or disease.

But even if you or all your friends and relatives are

whole and healthy, you still do not remain unaffected by the large disabled population in this country. Your kitchen mop may have been constructed by a sightless person, your car upholstered by a mentally retarded one, and your tax dollars could be going toward the warehousing of disabled individuals who are, by the nature of their confinement, being prevented from living as productive, contributing citizens.

Since it is no longer possible to avoid the issue of disability, since we cannot always turn our heads away in shame every time we come in contact with a disabled person, it is time we made an effort to understand their special problems. After all, our reactions of fear and repugnance are based on ignorance more than anything else. Knowledge and understanding are, therefore, the first steps on the road to acceptance. In this section we will be taking a realistic look at some of the more striking forms of physical disability—blindness, deafness, orthopedic defects and brain injury. We will learn about the causes of each, the limitations it places on its victims, and how many are able to overcome these limitations in order to fulfill their human potential.

Being Blind

Don't pity me. That's the worst thing you can do for a blind person!

BOB SORREL

Blindness is generally considered by the sighted to be the most severe handicap imaginable. When we try to imagine what a loss of vision would mean for us, we can think only of negative things—helplessness, total dependency on others, complete incapacitation and profound unhappiness. Fortunately, losing one's sight does not actually have to be such an extreme misfortune. Many sightless people lead relatively normal, independent lives. The only thing that stands in their way, aside from their loss of vision, is the false perception of their disability held by the majority of sighted people.

There are about 6.4 million Americans who suffer from some kind of vision impairment. There are many types and causes of such impairment. The most severely impaired—the legally blind—are the 1.7 million whose vision in the better eye is no better than 20/200, even with the use of a corrective lens. That means that they can see no more at a distance of 20 feet than a person with normal vision can see at 200 feet. Most so-called "blind" persons have some usable vision. Only 400,000 of the severely visually impaired have no usable vision to speak of. People who are born blind are known as congenitally blind, while those who become blind as a result of disease or accident are called adventitiously blind.

The greater portion of sightless people in the United States are over the age of sixty-five because the major causes of blindness are associated with diseases of the aging. Here are some of them.

Diabetic retinopathy is the leading cause of blindness in this country. It is a condition that affects some, although not all, diabetics in varying degrees of severity; vision is impaired as a result of the hemorrhaging of tiny blood vessels in the retina. *Cataracts* are the clouding of the normally clear lens of the eye. *Glaucoma* is a condition characterized by a gradual loss of sight, starting with peripheral vision. The end result is blindness, brought on by a buildup in the pressure of the fluid in the eye. *Retinitis pigmentosa* is an inherited condition that begins with a loss in night vision, then gradually progresses to the loss of side vision. In severe cases the result is total blindness. Finally, there is *macular degeneration,* which is a loss of vision that occurs primarily in the elderly. It is characterized by a loss of central vision and it is caused by damaged blood vessels in the macula, a part of the retina.

Although 65 per cent of the visually disabled people in this country are over sixty-five, there are approximately 60,000 blind children of school or preschool age. Just what effect does blindness have on the very young—those blind from birth or those blinded shortly thereafter, who have no real visual memories stored up? How might they differ from the sighted children around them?

In the first few months of life the sightless infant will appear quite normal—laughing, smiling, crying and generally making all the accepted facial expressions and body movements of the normal infant. But gradually it will become apparent that there is something wrong. This initial expressiveness will decrease rapidly because the infant lacks access to the visual stimuli that would encourage its development. In other words, he can't see people smiling back at him, and encouraging him to respond. He also cannot react to the colors and objects the normal child reaches out to grasp.

As the baby gets a little older other signs that all is not as it should be may become noticeable. Development of motor skills may seem retarded. The sightless infant does not usually sit, stand, crawl or walk as early as other children because, here again, he lacks the visual impetus to do so. In addition, his sense of balance may be affected by his impaired vision.

While his motor skills may seem to lag, his language capabilities may soar ahead of other children his age. Unless this tendency toward verbal precocity is carefully guided, it can degenerate into mere verbalism, or the manipulation of words that have no real meaning for the sightless child. (For example, a blind child may use the word "brown," but since he cannot experience colors the term remains essentially meaningless for him. The same thing holds true for the sighted person using the word "blind.")

The sightless child comes to rely heavily on his auditory sense for perception of the outside world. He may respond to strange or unexpected noises with fear and anxiety because, deprived of vision, sound becomes his only warning of possible danger. Touch also becomes very important, and he will tend to walk with arms outstretched, although this very normal reaction under the circumstances may be inhibited because of society's taboo against touching.

Because of his loss of this very important link with the outside world, the sightless child may become withdrawn. He may appear to lack the curiosity of other children, and instead of actively exploring his environment, he will be more likely to become preoccupied with himself and his own body. He may develop so-called "blindisms," which are repeated rhythmic movements for the purpose of self-stimulation, such as swaying, rocking, knocking the head with the hands, rubbing the eyes, etc. He may appear to be off in his own world, for as he comes to rely more and more on his own inner stimuli, he is likely to construct a rich fantasy life for himself.

At some point in early childhood, the sightless child will start to become aware of his difference, of the fact that he lacks an ability that those around him have. He will notice that he can't do certain things that others can. At first he might ascribe this superior ability to the fact that those who possess it are "grown up." But when he comes into contact with children his own age, who also possess this strange skill, he will know that something is missing. This early social interaction with children his own age is an important turning point in the development of any child. It is especially so for the sightless or visually impaired child, who is very sensitive to the way his peers react to him as he is developing an awareness of his difference.

If other children are cruel or tease him, he may feel threatened or rejected by those whose friendship he seeks. This may cause him to withdraw deeper into himself, and if this withdrawal is not checked by the love and encouragement of those close to him, the child may retreat so far from reality that it will be difficult or even impossible to bring him back. Omwake and Solnit in their study, "It Isn't Fair: The Treatment of a Blind Child," drew these conclusions about a blind girl named Ann:

> It is extraordinarily complicated for the child who becomes blind soon after birth to comprehend the absence of visual capacity that the sighted world takes for granted. In order to gain an impression of himself, his love objects, and the world in which he lives, a blind child depends more than the sighted child on all his other senses and the protection, guidance and interpretations of reality by his parents.

The profound confusion of the visually impaired child trying to come to grips with his disability is reflected in Ann's questioning:

> Why can't I write with my eyes? Why did I always want to touch my mother? Where does the loving go when the scolding comes in the voice? Can you see the echo come back? What color is it when it is blue?

It is especially important, therefore, for parents, teachers and the friends of the visually disabled child to work diligently to help him make a good adjustment. They should encourage his involvement in outside activities and help him to know that his disability need not prevent him from growing to independent adulthood. The overprotective parent or the parent who ignores his sight-impaired child's desires and feelings when making decisions which will affect his future development, may even seriously hamper his growth. According to Frumkin and Frumkin:

> From a psychological perspective, it is essential that the blind child develop a concept of himself which is a healthy and realistic one. The blind child must be made to realize that he has a handicap but that it is a handicap which does

not necessitate that he play throughout his life a deviant role, become an isolate, completely dependent, unemployable, etc. The individual's conception of his role and status is not rigidly determined by the degree of impairment of his vision. What is most significant is how he defines his role and status, what being blind means to him. So that blind children do not make a profession of dependency as blind adults, they must learn early in life the qualities of inpendence, self-reliance, etc., that make possible leading a relatively normal life in spite of the severe visual handicaps that they must live with.†

So it is the individual's concept of himself that is really more important than the disability, and it is up to those around the sight-impaired child to see to it that his self-image is a healthy one.

Adolescence is a particularly sensitive time for anyone. The years of passage from childhood to adulthood are highly stressful ones. It is a time when conformity to the standards set by one's peers is of ultimate importance, and any deviation from those standards can cause all kinds of emotional stress. These standards of conformity are especially significant in the area of physicality. Everyone is supposed to walk, talk and look essentially the same. For the visually impaired or sightless teen-ager this kind of strict conformity is quite impossible.

The resultant gap between the desire to belong and the impossibility of really belonging, because of one's physical differences, can be acutely stressful for the visually disabled teen-ager. Here again the desire to withdraw from society may manifest itself to a greater or lesser degree, depending upon the strength of earlier personal develop-

---

† Robert M. Frumkin and Miriam Ziesenwine Frumkin, "The Blind, Partially Seeing and Color Weak," in *The Unusual Child*, Joseph S. Reusch, ed., New York: Philosophical Library, 1962.

BEING BLIND 31

ment, and the attitude of the peer group. If his parents and loved ones have helped provide him with a sense of his own worth and an acceptance of his limitations, then this transition period need not be unbearably stressful.

If the vision-impaired youth receives the right training, he can go a long way toward overcoming many of the limitations of his disability. As noted earlier, there are only about 400,000 persons who are without any visual perception whatsoever. The rest of the visually impaired can learn to make optimum use of whatever residual vision they may have, whether it be full peripheral vision or only the recognition of lightness and darkness.

There are many personal and educational aids available to the vision-impaired individual. We have all seen the guide dogs and canes that help sightless people increase their mobility. For those who cannot read the "fine print" of most books and publications there are books reprinted in bold type, and special high-intensity magnifiers are available. Some books have been recorded on long-playing records.

Perhaps the single most important educational tool ever developed for the blind is the Braille system of touch reading and writing in which raised dots are combined in formations that represent the letters of the alphabet. Before the development of this system in 1824 by Louis Braille, sightless people had no satisfactory means of printed communication, and it was quite impossible for the average sightless person to get an adequate education. Today many books are available in Braille. However, the supply of Braille books, along with other educational aids for the partially sighted in this country, still lags woefully behind the need.

With proper training the sightless and the vision-impaired can learn to develop their other senses in such a way as to compensate in part for their visual loss. It is quite a widespread belief that the sightless or other sensorily impaired individuals are automatically compensated by nature for the loss of one sense with the increased effectiveness of the others. However, recent studies have found that this is just not so—that this belief is no more than wishful thinking on the part of those who would like to be relieved of their social responsibilities to the disabled.

In fact, quite the opposite can occur. If not properly stimulated, the sightless child could become quite backward in sensory development. But if guided and stimulated, he can develop astounding sensory capabilities, particularly in the auditory and tactile areas.

This leads us to another popular myth: Blind people are innately more musically inclined than most people. In fact, the spread of natural musical ability among the sightless population is no more intense than that of the normal. But, here again, if given the opportunity, the sightless individual with musical talent and a highly developed auditory sense, who is willing to work long and hard, is likely to make great strides in the world of music. It is one more ability that should be nurtured.

Despite the progress of education programs designed to serve visually disabled children in this country, only a fraction of those in need receive the benefits of superior training, and no amount of education, training and personal adjustment can assure the visually impaired individual social acceptance or employment when he reaches adulthood anyway.

Most sighted people react to the sightless with a mixture

of embarrassment and pity. They feel sorry for the blind person they see approaching a crosswalk and they want to help him get across safely. What most sighted people fail to understand is that if a blind person is walking on the street alone, he is most likely quite capable of getting around on his own and doesn't want to be pushed or pulled around by us. He will ask for it if he feels he needs assistance.

What he really needs—a decent job—sighted people are reluctant to offer. A visually disabled adult does not want to be constantly reminded of his dependency on the sighted. He wants to feel he can pull his own weight in society, not that he must be pushed, pulled or dragged along by the sighted. As Frumkin and Frumkin comment:

> There is too much of a tendency in our culture to pity the blind instead of trying to understand the nature of their handicap. This pity has taken the form of humanitarian programs which too often lead to greater rather than lesser dependence, increases rather than decreases the social distance between the blind and sighted, and tends to perpetuate stereotypes of the blind that interfere with their fullest participation in society.

What sighted people can't believe is that blind people can take care of themselves and be relatively independent working people. As Morris Goret, a successful real estate broker who was blinded in mid-career, quite matter-of-factly put it: "I can do everything and anything I did before, except see." But because the sighted are reluctant to accept this as true, blind people are forced to prove themselves better at what they do than the average sighted person in order to gain any sort of recognition. This puts an unfair responsibility on the shoulders of the visually disabled person, but it is one very many have cheerfully accepted, and their achievements over and again give the lie to the fears and misgivings of the sighted.

Kathy Larsen, a blind medical transcriber, says: "I feel it's up to blind people that have a capability to show other people that blind people are not helpless and that they can do things. The average person is uneducated as to what any handicapped person can do." Kathy and many, many sight-impaired people would probably agree with Bob Sorrel, the former rancher blinded by a gunshot who is now a successful art framer and cabinetmaker, quoted at the beginning of this section, who declares emphatically, "Blindness is not a handicap!"

Many great people of history were blinded at some point during their lives, and their work hardly suffered as a result of their disability. The Greek poet Homer, mentioned earlier, was blind. John Milton, one of the greatest poets of the English language, wrote one of his most enduring works, *Paradise Lost*, after a disease, probably glaucoma, left him totally blind. A controversial figure in seventeenth-century England and often under attack for the beliefs expressed in his works, Milton wrote quite eloquently of his blindness in answer to his critics:

> I neither believe nor feel myself an object of God's anger, but actually experience and acknowledge His fatherly mercy and kindness to me in all matters of greatest moment . . . If the choice were necessary, I would prefer my blindness to yours—yours is a cloud spread over the mind, which darkens both the light of reason and conscience; mine keeps from my view only the colored surface of things, while it leaves me liberty to contemplate the stability of virtue and truth.

Denis Diderot, the French philosopher and scholar, published a book in 1749, titled *Letters on the Blind for the Use of Thou Who See*, in which he revealed to the public for the first time the personalities and the extraordinary accomplishments of several blind persons.

In many ancient cultures the blind were revered, and held positions of honor. There were so many blind people functioning as full citizens in Egypt that the Greek poet Hesiod called it the "country of the blind," and the Greek historian Herodotus recorded the fame of Egyptian oculists. In India, Buddhist monks erected hospitals for the blind, and early Hindu medical books list seventy-six eye disorders. In China there were blind soothsayers and keepers of the oral tradition. Perhaps the most important position held by blind people in the ancient world was that of prophet, or "seer." In ancient Greece and Rome, men like the blind prophets Phineas and Tiresias were honored because it was believed that the blind were especially suited to prophecy.

> The extraordinary development of the remaining senses, the lessened contact with the outer world, the more marked development of introspection which renders the blind person more finely sensitive—all were believed to bring the blind into a closer communion with the supernatural. The primary asset of this union was the ability to foresee the future.‡

In this instance a sightless person's disability was seen as a positive asset rather than a liability. The loss of the distracting sense of vision was seen as an aid to the attainment of wisdom and insight. When they paid homage to the

‡ French, Richard Slayton, *From Homer to Helen Keller, A Social and Educational Study of the Blind*. New York: American Foundation for the Blind, Inc., 1932.

blind, these ancient peoples were acknowledging the fact that blind people had unique talents and abilities to offer society.

Today, there is hardly a profession or trade that does not include at least one blind person. There are blind lawyers, doctors, teachers, nuclear physicists, college professors, social workers, musicians, artists, sculptors, at least one television newscaster and a United States Senator (Thomas Gore of Oklahoma). New York State had its first blind Supreme Court Justice in 1975. Judge Gilberto Ramirez' brilliant career was discussed in a December 13, 1975 New York *Times* article, that concluded:

> Judge Ramirez feels that his handicap does not interfere with his rendering fair decisions. Instead, he says seeing defendants can sometimes be "misleading."
>
> "Cockiness may be a coverup," he says, "or a frightened person may be a truthful person. I have no problem picking that up."

William Schmidt, a high school principal, like the Judge, feels that his blindness may be an asset in his line of work. He says: "I really feel strongly that in many ways blindness has been an asset rather than a liability. I think it's caused me to be a better teacher. I have to plan more carefully. I have to rely a great deal on students' self-control, self-discipline . . ."

Joe McDonagh, a farmer who is blind, comments good-naturedly: "My calves do not realize it, but my cows know I am blind as well as I do, but they never take unfair advantage of their knowledge."

Psychologists, electrical engineers, computer programmers, factory workers—the list of achievements of blind working men and women is nearly endless. The sightless also participate in all the sports, including skiing, riding, bowling, golfing, swimming and so on. As the blind scholar and pioneer psychologist Pierre Villey wrote in his great work, *The World of the Blind,* "Before anything else it is necessary to establish the fundamental truth that blindness does not affect the individuality but leaves it intact. Its sources remain healthy; no mental faculty of the blind is affected in any way, and all of them, under favorable circumstances are susceptible of blooming out to the highest degree of development to which a normal being can aspire."

We would do well to remember the words of Pierre Villey the next time we meet a sightless person, and to remember the great strides many blind people have made in spite of the negative and often discouraging attitudes of the sighted toward them. Try to imagine how much more sightless people could achieve in an atmosphere of respect, acceptance and active encouragement the next time you have the opportunity to influence the life of a visually impaired person. When next you meet at the crosswalk, at school, at work, think of who he is and what he can do. Look at him simply as a person not as a "blind" person. If you treat him with dignity, he won't disappoint you.

Being Deaf

> Ours is not the silence that soothes the weary senses. It is an inhuman silence which severs and estranges. It is a silence which isolates cruelly and completely. Hearing is the deepest, most humanizing, philosophical sense man possesses.
>
> HELEN KELLER

Take a moment now to listen. Listen to the sounds that make up your aural environment. If you are sitting alone at home in a quiet room absorbed in reading, you might not be fully aware of all the sounds you are picking up right now. Just listen for a moment and you will be surprised at the number of sounds you hear. Listen as a plane buzzes overhead; a bird sings outside your window; someone runs water in the tub in the bathroom upstairs; a dog howls in the distance; floor boards creak in the next room; a door slams; a voice calls; the paper crackles as you turn the pages of this book.

These are but a few of the sounds that make up the aural environment you have come to take for granted, the comfortably familiar sounds of your surroundings. And don't forget the other meaningful sounds that speak to you throughout your lifetime: the jarring sounds that warn you to be careful at a busy intersection; the soothing sounds of a seaside vacation; the cacophony of sounds that bring an amusement park to life; the pleasing sounds of your favorite music—all the thousands of sounds that we hear in a lifetime and that lend an added richness and variety to everything we do.

Imagine, if you can, that you are sitting right where you are only now you are engulfed in absolute silence. It is difficult to imagine, since none of us who have normal hearing has ever experienced a total sound vacuum. No matter how quiet you may think it is, there are always sounds making their way into your auditory system, even when you are asleep. (Remember lying asleep and dreaming about a phone ringing, only to awaken and find it *is* ringing?)

The only thing that comes close to the experience of total silence for the average person would be, perhaps, the experience of floating nearly motionless underwater. It is an eerie but not unpleasant sensation, to feel totally cut off from the noisy world above the surface. But imagine if you had to remain cut off like that for the rest of your life, if you had to remain forever isolated from all the familiar sounds that bring you information, comfort and pleasure, doomed to watch the world as if it were an endless silent movie, without titles.

This is the case for the more than a quarter million Americans who are profoundly deaf, and in varying degrees for the more than 20 million—that's approximately one in ten—who have some kind of hearing impairment. Included in this number are the more than 3 million children who suffer from some degree of hearing loss. Each of these people is to a greater or lesser extent cut off from the solace of sound. They cannot hear the continuous noises of day-to-day life that the rest of us take for granted and hear only half-consciously. Noise is of great psychological importance and means for the normally hearing that life is going on and that they are in touch with other living beings. Noise reassures us. The deaf do not have that same reassurance. Their world is silent, and silence leads to isolation.

All sound is produced by the vibration of air particles. These vibrations are carried by the air to the eardrum of the listener, who then perceives an auditory sensation; that is, the listener *hears* the sound. If the sound sensation is somehow blocked in the ear itself and cannot, in fact, be heard, the ear is said to be deaf. Some children are congenitally deaf, being born without hearing. Deafness in this case is either inherited or caused by some prenatal difficulty such as the contraction of German measles by the mother during pregnancy. Others lose their hearing later on as a result of accident or disease. Measles, scarlet fever, and other viral diseases as well as meningitis, encephalitis and bacterial infections are some of the common illnesses that may lead to deafness. Even the common cold, if not properly cared for, can lead to infections of the ear which, in turn, can cause deafness.

There are two kinds of deafness. One is called conductive deafness. It is caused by a mechanical blockage in the hearing path, such as excessive wax, fluid in the middle ear, an abscess or a perforation of the eardrum. Medical removal of the blockage can often restore full or partial hearing. The other kind of deafness is called nerve deafness. In this case, the sensitive tissues of the inner ear or the auditory nerve have either failed to develop properly or have been irreparably damaged. There is no remedy or treatment for this kind of deafness, although a hearing aid often restores partial hearing.

In some cases the effect of this damage is uneven. A condition known as high-tone deafness can occur, in which a child is unable to hear the higher sound frequencies but can hear sounds in the lower ranges. This is very difficult to detect, because the child will appear to hear sometimes and not at others. He may eventually grow to ignore all sound because the low tones without the high become meaningless.

Another condition, *aphasia*, is often confused with deafness. In this case, however, there is no damage or blockage in the ear. The ear remains intact, and the person suffering from aphasia can in fact hear. But some damage to the brain prevents sound from having any meaning. The aphasiac child can hear, but he is unable to understand what he hears as a result of this brain injury. Since sound is, therefore, meaningless to him, he soon comes to totally disregard what he hears. He eventually becomes so skillful at ignoring sound that he appears incapable of hearing.

Like the blind infant, the congenitally deaf baby will appear normal in his initial development. He will make the usual gurgling sounds and may even progress to the babbling stage. Many doctors consider this early babbling instinctive, like sucking and chewing. But instead of moving forward in the development of speech, the deaf baby, because of the vacuum of sound in which he lives, will gradually regress and become nearly silent. Since he cannot adequately hear the sounds of those speaking to him, he is unable to imitate those sounds, and the development of speech is therefore retarded.

This inability to imitate sounds because they cannot be heard is more often than not the only cause of the muteness that is associated with deafness. This muteness is, therefore, a learning problem rather than a physical one. Because speech is not automatic and normally must be learned through listening and constant repetition, teaching the deaf child to speak is extremely difficult.

Finding an alternate means of communication becomes, therefore, the central problem of the deaf child's life. Since he cannot hear words, he quite naturally does not know they exist. This does not mean, however, that he lacks the ability to understand symbolic language or hasn't the desire to communicate. He can think and conceptualize just as the normal child, but since he does not hear the common language and hence cannot use it, he will develop his own private symbolic code made up of pantomime, gestures or drawings that represent his feelings and thoughts.

As he moves into contact with other children and people outside the immediate circle of his family who love and understand him, the hearing-impaired child is likely to experience frustration because of his inability to communicate in the normal accepted verbal way. He will feel isolated and out of place because he cannot master the language that brings people together. He may feel rejected if he is ostracized or ridiculed by his peers, who find his first crude attempts at verbalization funny or queer. Children who suffer from speech disorders such as stuttering, or those resulting from cerebral palsy, abnormal dentition, or harelip are subject to the same embarrassment over their initial attempts to speak.

It is quite obvious that if the deaf child is to participate fully in the normal world he must acquire a means of bridging the verbal communication gap, but since the beginnings of the movement to give the deaf child special training in the communication skills he so desperately needs, there has been a heated controversy over which of two opposing methods of instruction should prevail—the strictly oral or the manual, which uses sign language and finger-spelling.

Within the last century or so the oral method has maintained its position as the preferred method. During this time it became the widely accepted belief that the deaf child should be taught to communicate orally through intensive speech therapy, which made use of lip-reading, sound amplification and vibration. Any use of manual or sign language was forbidden in an effort to make deaf children communicate just like hearing ones, or at least appear to.

Recent studies have found, however, that this overemphasis on the strictly oral aspect of language and communication has had some very negative effects on those it was supposed to help. It has often led deaf children to have some very negative feelings about themselves and their disability, to believe that their hearing loss was somehow wrong or bad and something therefore to be hidden or denied. As they struggled to hear through their eyes and to approximate speech through feeling its sounds, so that they might seem more like everyone else, they were more often than not doomed to failure.

Lip-reading is an extremely difficult technique to master. In the English language, where more than half the sounds are hemophenous (they look like some other sound when formed on the lips), satisfactory lip-reading becomes nearly impossible. Very few deaf people are ever able to understand speech through this means alone. In addition few deaf people are ever able to develop speech that is acceptable to the normal population.

This oral elitism of the normally hearing in the education of the deaf which demanded that everyone communicate in the one standard acceptable fashion has begun gradually to lose ground in recent years under the pressure of overwhelming evidence that a combination of the two formerly competing methods, the oral and the manual—known as "total communication"—is more effective. By using sign language to fill in the gaps in lip-reading, the child gets a more solid grounding in the structure of language and is thus able to communicate and verbalize more effectively.

As one famed pediatrician, Dr. Arnold Gesell, wrote in the *Volta Review*, twenty years ago: "Our aim should not be to convert the deaf child into a somewhat fictitious version of a normal hearing child, but into a well-adjusted nonhearing child who is completely managing the limitations of his sensory defect."

No matter how well he learns the language, the deaf person's use of it will always differ to a greater or lesser degree from the norm, and unless the hearing are willing to overcome their squeamishness at his strange signs and halting speech—unless they are willing to meet him halfway—he will continue to be isolated behind a "sound barrier." At least one counselor of the deaf has made the following request:

> I would say the greatest service you . . . can bestow on the deaf is to learn to understand us and then teach others to understand us. What this means, first of all, is that we must break that "sound barrier." To do that you will have to learn to talk to us in our own language of signs, for most of us cannot possibly learn to talk to you in yours. Or you must learn to form your words on your lips the way they

should be formed so the more fortunate lip-reading deaf have a better chance to understand you. Above all, never show irritation or impatience when we cannot seem to grasp what you are saying.*

Unfortunately, it is not likely that the majority of hearing people will heed these words, for the deaf are no different from any other disabled minority when it comes to the depth of the prejudice of the normal. Modern prejudice against the deaf has its roots in ancient times. A faulty interpretation of the Greek philosopher Aristotle's expression of what were in his day very advanced beliefs regarding the deaf greatly influenced popular judgment for centuries thereafter.

He declared: "Those born deaf all become speechless. They have a voice but are destitute of speech." This appears to be an accurate assessment of the relationship of muteness to deafness, but his statement came to be interpreted quite differently over the centuries. In Greek the word for "speechless" is also the same for "senseless," i.e., without sense or reason. Aristotle's original intention becomes irrelevant in light of the misinterpretation that was accepted as fact for hundreds of years—that the deaf were mental incompetents.

The poet Lucretius wrote: "To instruct the deaf no art could ever reach/No care improve, no wisdom teach." Ancient Hebraic and Roman law classed the deaf as incapable, along with children, lunatics and fools, and required the deaf to be placed under special guardians who acted in their behalf in legal matters. The early Christians later

---

* Don Pettingell, "Adjustments of the Deaf," address before workshop: "Understanding the Deaf Client," at University of Colorado, July 14–15, 1964, printed in *Deaf Adults*, a National Association of the Deaf publication.

adopted the belief that the deaf were uneducable, which is especially curious in light of the fact that many early orders of Christian monks operated under a strict vow of silence and as a result developed very intricate manual sign languages. The fact that no one ever thought to teach this sign language to the deaf is a testimony to the strength of the fallacy of deaf incompetence. So the deaf remained outcasts, ignored and doomed to live in unenlightened silence for many hundreds of years.

Today these ancient and totally unfounded prejudices still linger, albeit in more subtle forms, in spite of the fact that modern intelligence tests, which do not require the use of language, have established that the distribution of intelligence among the deaf approximates that of the normal. Today deaf people are often refused the right to rent a house or apartment because landlords consider them incapable of maintaining a residence; and many deaf people are found in jobs far inferior to their abilities. Many employers refuse to hire deaf people at all because they are not able to use a regular telephone and require assistance in a job where the use of the telephone is necessary.

A more likely reason why employers show reluctance to hire the deaf is that they fear their employees who can hear will resent the fact that a deaf person can do the work as well as they. Like other disabled people trying to make it in a normal world that is reluctant to accept them, the deaf have to work doubly hard to prove themselves and must have endless patience and understanding in dealing with the prejudices of the normal. The deaf person knows that the reactions of the normal are unfounded, and he has the added burden of educating them to the reality of his true capabilities.

All of us have to prove our capabilities on the job, but most of us benefit from the fact that employers and fellow workers are willing to believe in us and give us a reasonable chance to do the job, to let us stand innocent until proven guilty of incompetence. For the deaf person the opposite is more often than not the case. He is considered guilty in the face of our prejudice before he even goes on trial in the work place and must achieve better than his co-workers in order to prove he is equal to the task.

In spite of the tremendous odds against them, the deaf have proven themselves many times over throughout history. Deaf people are found in all walks of life, in both skilled and unskilled work. There are deaf lawyers, doctors, architects, teachers, ministers, photographers and engineers; there are deaf mechanics, watchmakers, machinists, woodworkers and upholsterers.

Ludwig van Beethoven, recognized as a musical genius and one of the greatest composers ever to have lived, suffered from an ear disease that gradually brought him to total deafness. After becoming completely deaf in 1818 he went on to compose some of his most memorable works, including his immortal *Ninth Symphony*.

Juan Fernan Havenette, the sixteenth-century painter, known as the "Spanish Titian," was deaf, and the sixteenth-century French poet Pierre de Ronsard had a hearing problem that did not adversely affect his literary output. His friend and fellow poet, who also happened to be deaf, Joachim du Bellay dedicated his *"Hymne à la Surdité"* to him, in which he said:

> I will say that to be deaf—for those who know
> The difference between good and evil (they are few)—
> Is not an evil, only seems to be so.

The contemporary poet, David Wright, who has been deaf since childhood, wrote about his disability in his poem "Monologue of a Deaf Man":

> The injury, dominated, is an asset:
> It is there for the domination, that is all.

Many prominent figures in the arts, sports and politics have suffered from hearing losses and have overcome them. Among these are Larry Brown, pro football's Most Valuable Player in 1972; U. S. Senators Vance Hartke and Charles Percy; the late Academy Award-winning actor Fredric March; and George C. Wallace, Governor of Alabama and three-time presidential candidate.

There are even award-winning troops of deaf actors and mimes who tour the United States and Europe. David Hays, the director of the National Theater of the Deaf, argues that the deaf actor actually has many advantages that the hearing actor does not:

> Usually, you get a good voice or a good body, but not necessarily both in the same person . . . In the deaf actor, the voice is the body. He speaks with his body—I mean the actual words made with his hands—and it makes him a vastly better actor. There is a unity between body and speech. Speech comes from the very center of the deaf actor. He has spent his whole life in an effort to communicate.

As a proof of his belief, Mr. Hays contrasted the ability to communicate of the deaf actors and the hearing ones on a tour in Yugoslavia. None of the actors spoke Serbo-Croation, the local language. When they went to purchase some toothpaste at a drugstore, "The deaf actors had no trouble getting the idea across, but the others did."

Communication is the key to unlocking the isolation of

the deaf and hard of hearing, but it is obvious that the deaf person cannot communicate if we are not willing to listen. Communication is dialogue, it is interraction, it is understanding. Consider this all too typical experience of a deaf person in a hearing world:

> Imagine a deaf person in a group of hearing people. It is uncomfortable enough just sitting there in silence, trying to look wise, with plenty of time to think and speculate. The hearing people cannot help but be aware of the presence of the deaf person. Glances are directed inadvertently or self-consciously at him. Someone cracks a joke and everyone else laughs. More glances. The deaf person turns to his neighbor and asks what's so funny. With the conversation still going, and interesting, the neighbor does not want to be distracted just then, or he does not know how to explain without going into the over-all subject in order to make sense, or he just doesn't want to be bothered. So, with something like, "Oh it wasn't anything, really," or "I'll tell you later," or any number of excuses that the deaf naturally have to accept he lamely dismisses it. I am not exaggerating. Such an incident happens so often that the deaf avoid such a situation if they can; when they can't, it is hard to keep from lapsing back into silence and becoming resentful and suspicious. Anyone would!

It is up to us, therefore, to overcome our prejudices and our impatience with the deaf and hard of hearing and to take the time to listen to what they have to say. It is not such a difficult thing really. It doesn't take that much longer to converse with the deaf, and the potential rewards are well worth the effort. The person who takes time to listen carefully and respond intelligibly to the deaf, cannot help but improve his own ability to communicate.

Neurological Dysfunctions—
Brain and Nerve Disorders

The human nervous system is made up of the brain, the spinal cord and an intricate network of nerves that reaches throughout the entire body. The brain controls all bodily functions through the signals it sends via the nerves. When brain and nerve tissue is healthy, the body functions normally. But if this tissue is injured or damaged in some way, the complex communication system will break down and result in physical dysfunction of varying degrees. There are more than two hundred known neurological disorders, and approximately 20 million Americans suffer from one or more of them. They account for 20 per cent of the hospitalizations and 12 per cent of the deaths in this country in a year.

Neurological dysfunctions manifest themselves in a variety of ways, depending upon the location and severity of the damage to the nervous system. Causes vary, but are generally held in common by all the different disorders. That is to say, one cause may trigger a variety of different neurological failures. The most prominent causes of brain injuries can be divided into three categories. There are those occurring before birth or during the birth process, which include hereditary or congenital causes, RH blood incompatability between the mother and the child she is carrying, infections or diseases such as German measles in the pregnant mother, X rays during pregnancy, placental separation, premature birth, birth delay, protracted labor or difficult birth, or a break in the oxygen supply to the baby's brain before, during or directly after birth.

The second group would include those accidental causes occurring at any stage of development after birth, such as head or spinal-cord injury, or poisoning.

The third comprises diseases and physiological conditions that may affect the nervous system of the child or adult, including encephalitis, meningitis, measles, malnutrition, stroke, brain tumor, and the degeneration of tissue associated with old age.

There are some dysfunctions—multiple sclerosis and muscular dystrophy are two of the more well-known—for which there is no known cause. There is no cure for brain injury, although many symptoms can be partially alleviated through medical treatment or physiotherapy. In this section we will be examining some of the more widespread and apparent of the disabling neurological dysfunctions, including epilepsy, cerebral palsy, multiple sclerosis, muscular dystrophy and mental retardation.

Epilepsy

The word epilepsy applies to a number of disorders of the nervous system, so it would be more precise to say "the epilepsies." These disorders are characterized by sudden seizures that result from a build-up of excessive electrical charges in the cells of the brain. The seizures are characterized by muscular convulsions, loss of consciousness and temporary mental confusion or disturbance of bodily functions. These symptoms occur with a greater or lesser de-

NEUROLOGICAL DYSFUNCTIONS

gree of severity, depending upon the amount of electrical discharge and its location in the brain. There are three major types of epileptic seizures.

Grand mal, perhaps the most physically dramatic of the three, can occur with varying degrees of frequency. Usually of a minute or more duration, it is characterized by blackouts, violent muscular convulsions that can affect most of the body, and irregular breathing; after the seizure is over the person may feel confused and drowsy, and will probably need to sleep for a number of hours.

Petit mal is the form most common in children between the ages of six and fourteen. It is characterized by many mini-seizures—as many as a hundred in a single day—usually only of a few seconds duration. The visible signs of the petit-mal seizure are staring, rapid blinking, and some possible muscle twitching. The individual is rarely aware that he has experienced a seizure after he comes out of it.

Psychomotor is perhaps the most complex form of seizure. It affects persons of all ages, lasts anywhere from a few seconds to many hours and manifests itself in a variety of bizarre and purposeless actions, such as: hand rubbing, sensations of ringing in the ears, dizziness, spots before the eyes, headaches and unexplained displays of strong emotions such as fear, anger, rage. Often the patient cannot remember what has occurred during the seizure and will need to sleep afterward.

In many cases, doctors are unable to find any traceable cause for the epileptic seizures. In this case the seizures are termed *idiopathic*. When a cause has been found the epilepsy is called *symptomatic*. It is estimated that at least 4 million Americans have epilepsy, that is one in every fifty persons, or more than all those who have cancer, tuberculosis, cerebral palsy, multiple sclerosis and muscular dystrophy combined.

Although there is no cure for epilepsy, seizures can be more or less controlled through the use of anticonvulsant drugs. At least 50 per cent of those suffering from epilepsy can attain total seizure control, and another 30 per cent are able to benefit from partial control. Contrary to widespread belief, epilepsy is not contagious or necessarily handicapping, and it is most definitely not a mental illness, although some of its symptoms may resemble those of mental disorders. In addition, epileptics have been found to have the same range of intelligence as other people, although in some cases, early uncontrolled seizures may affect mental ability. Epilepsy need not, therefore, necessarily prevent an individual from leading a full and productive life.

In spite of these facts, societal attitudes and prejudices regarding epilepsy haven't yet emerged from the dark ages. The word epilepsy comes from the Greek word meaning "to be seized," and it was believed that the epileptic was seized by demons. Epilepsy was known as the "dark disorder" in some cultures, although others recognized it as the "sacred disease."

The latter designation would seem more appropriate considering some of the more prominent historical figures believed to have been epileptics—Alexander the Great, Buddha, Socrates, Julius Caesar, St. Paul, Napoleon, Handel, Dante, Tchaikovsky and Alfred Nobel. It is understandable that the ancients were confused by the rather odd behavior of epileptics, and that they sought explanations for it in the supernatural. But given the medical facts as they are known today, there is no excuse for the fear and prejudice against epileptics that still prevails.

It is society's low regard for him that is the epileptic's real handicap. The effect of this ignorant prejudice can be devastating, especially for the epileptic child. "Children with epilepsy are often the brunt of discrimination and prejudice. Their classmates unwittingly subject them to humiliation, isolation and rejection when they don't understand epilepsy and when they reflect the attitudes of uninformed adults. The stigma attached to this disorder can affect youngsters in school and continue to frustrate them socially, psychologically and economically throughout their lives."†

The experience of a teen-age boy who suffered from *grand-mal* epilepsy illustrates the anguish and guilt an adolescent may suffer as a result of fear of societal condemnation. Bill's parents felt forced to move the family to a new town every time their son's epilepsy became known. They tried to keep it a secret, but inevitably an unexpected seizure at school would blow Bill's cover and he'd ". . . just [want] to crawl away and die" from shame and embarrassment. Bill longed to be freed of the burden of his secret and to be accepted by others.

> I could put up with everything else if I just didn't have to sneak around all the time. I even think I wouldn't have so many seizures if I could just quit worrying about it, and my doctor says that I might be right about that.
>
> You know what I would like? I would like it if everybody could just go ahead and *know* I have epilepsy and not even care. I would just like to know what it feels like to be treated like everybody else. Not special. And not like I'm

† *Epilepsy School Alert,* pamphlet, Epilepsy Foundation of America, Washington, D.C., November 1973.

some kind of a monster or even like a baby that has to be taken care of all the time. But like a *person*.

I keep hoping that someday more people will understand what epilepsy is like, and then they won't have so much trouble being friends, or just accepting us as ordinary people. Sure, I'm a little different. But I'm not *that* different!‡

Unfortunately there remain innumerable obstacles preventing the 4 million Americans who, like Bill, suffer from prejudice against epileptics, from being accepted as "ordinary people." Among these obstacles are discriminatory legislation (some states have laws on the books that authorize sterilization of epileptics); discriminatorily high auto, health and life insurance rates; discriminatory employment practices attributable to employer apprehension, employee resistance and prejudicial workman's compensation laws; inadequate training and guidance for employable epileptics and uninformed public attitude.

Epilepsy, though one of the earliest known maladies of man, remains one of the least understood. The cloud that continues to shroud epilepsy prompted the great Supreme Court Justice Oliver Wendell Holmes to declare: "If I wished to show a student the difficulties of getting a truth from medical experience, I would give him the history of epilepsy to read." Through anticonvulsant drugs and other therapies, medical science has been able to bring some light and hope to those who suffer from the "dark disorder," but in spite of these great strides in the treatment of epileptics society remains fixed in its prejudice, and determined to keep epileptics in the dark.

A 1973 survey conducted by the Epilepsy Foundation of America among parents of epileptics rated lack of social

‡ *Epilepsy: A Teenager's View*, Epilepsy Foundation of America, Washington, D.C., n.d.

acceptance as one of the gravest handicaps facing their children, and over one half agreed that epilepsy would definitely affect their child's future career choice. It is known that people with epilepsy suffer fewer seizures if they are allowed to lead active, productive lives. It is also known that the psychological strain placed upon epileptics as a result of the obstacles to personal development created by society's ignorance and prejudice can be more disabling than the disorder itself. It is time society stopped heedlessly handicapping the epileptic with its prejudices and let him live the kind of life his own capabilities will dictate.

Cerebral Palsy

Like epilepsy, the term cerebral palsy refers to a number of related disorders. It is a group of medical conditions—not a disease—that are a result of damage to or malformation of the part of the brain that controls and co-ordinates muscular activity. "Cerebral" refers to the brain, and "palsy" (paralysis) to a lack of muscle control. Cerebral palsy ordinarily appears in infancy or early childhood and is characterized by involuntary, jerky movements, muscular spasticity and poor balance. Certain other physical anomalies, such as seizures, hearing and visual impairment, abnormal sensation and mental retardation often further complicate the condition.

There are three main types of cerebral palsy: *spastic*, characterized by stiff, difficult movements; *athetoid*, marked by involuntary and uncontrolled movements; and *ataxic*, characterized by a disturbed sense of balance and depth perception.

About 750,000 Americans have cerebral palsy, more

than 250,000 of whom are under twenty-one. An estimated 15,000 infants are born each year with this condition, for which there is no known cure. At present, treatment of cerebral palsy is limited to the alleviation of its symptoms via physical therapy, speech therapy, braces, orthopedic surgery and drug therapy used to relieve muscle tension and control seizures where indicated.

Cerebral palsy can often be detected in the infant within the first few months of life. The cerebral palsied baby appears to be abnormally slow in his development of muscular control. From the very beginning the baby may have trouble feeding. This is because he has difficulty co-ordinating the muscles used in sucking and swallowing. The baby becomes tense and irritable because he is frustrated in the act of feeding and usually not receiving proper nourishment as a result. This early stress is a foreshadowing of the difficulties that lie ahead for the cerebral palsied child, and it may possibly handicap his later emotional growth.

At about three or four months old the normal baby begins to lift his head in order better to observe his environment. He reaches out and grasps at bright, moving objects. The cerebral palsied baby is not able to control his head movements in this manner. His head lolls or is drawn in, and he may miss this early stimulation.

At five or six months the normal baby uses his hands and mouth in exploration of his environment. The cerebral palsied baby, especially the severely spastic, doesn't have this kind of motor control, and may become retarded in his judgment of objects as a result. His power of concentration falls behind in development because of his lack of sustained environmental stimulation. Since his capacity for

NEUROLOGICAL DYSFUNCTIONS

exploration is so limited, he is not able to sustain enjoyment with one toy, and is easily distracted.

Later on, when the normal baby is learning to sit and crawl, and then to stand and walk, the cerebral palsied infant lags far behind because his muscle development is so retarded. Learning to speak may be extremely difficult for the cerebral palsied child. His lack of muscle control can cause him to have great trouble breathing and using his tongue and vocal muscles effectively, all of which are essential to speech production. In addition, he may have a hearing problem that might further complicate his learning to speak.

By the time he reaches one year of age, the cerebral palsied child may appear dull, apathetic and uninterested in his surroundings, and his condition may seem hopeless to those around him. But that need not be the case. Trapped inside that unresponsive body there is a mind and a spirit that is waiting to be freed from its physical limitations. That is why it is so important to recognize the symptoms of cerebral palsy early in the child's life. With proper therapy the severity of the disability can be reduced and unhealthy or destructive behavior patterns can be altered.

"The part of the brain which controls the movement of the muscles has been damaged by the illness, and the child's muscles have to be re-educated to move in the right way. Left to himself, the child would choose the easiest way, using the strongest muscles and letting the weaker ones atrophy."*

The world can be a very frightening place for the cerebral palsied child. His lack of muscle control can leave him

---

* Bowley, Agatha H., *The Young Handicapped Child*, Edinburgh: E & S Livingstone, Ltd., 1957, p. 59.

with a feeling of helplessness. He is bound to experience many fears and frustrations in his daily existence. A fear of falling, for example, is quite natural under the circumstances, since his muscle weakness prevents him from protecting himself in that event. In the face of all this, his great need for a sense of security in his surroundings is understandable. Any sudden change in routine can be quite threatening and upsetting for the cerebral palsied child.

Under these conditions the cerebral palsied child's family and friends may very well be tempted to protect and spoil him, to cater to his fears, to fetch and carry for him without making any demands upon him. But catering to a child's dictates—any child's, but most especially the severely handicapped—is the worst thing that can be done for him. Such oversolicitousness only produces a pampered, self-indulgent tyrant whose emotional and physical growth are forever stunted. No one would argue that the cerebral palsied child is in need of special care, but this care should be focused on molding him into an independent adult, rather than keeping him a perpetually dependent child.

The best way to alleviate the cerebral palsied child's very real fears is not to protect him from them but to remove, as much as possible, their cause by encouraging him to gain better muscle control through physical therapy, letting him discover what he can for himself without interference and allowing him to achieve his potential. He should not be sheltered from life, but prompted to seek it out and experience it as fully as he is able. Success is the best medicine for the cerebral palsied child.

More than half the cerebral palsied children test within the normal range of intelligence, but because of their acute disabilities, their intellectual development may take much longer than the average. They have the ability, but the physical conditions prevent them from progressing quite as fast as others. Fortunately, the disabilities associated with cerebral palsy do not usually worsen with time. Once cerebral palsy's effects have been set, there is little change as the child grows, and with special training, he can be taught to live successfully within his limitations.

Tremendous patience and imagination are needed in the education of the cerebral palsied child. Because he is forced to remain largely sedentary, he needs a learning situation that will enhance and enrich his necessarily limited experience; and he needs the guidance of those willing to let him take his time to do things in his own unique way. He does not want or need pity or pampering. He wants to be understood and accepted for what he is, and appreciated for what he can do.

A number of cerebral palsied people are able to master their disability to the point where they can lead relatively normal lives when given the chance. But because of the particularly visible manifestations of their disability, and the striking originality of some of the means found to overcome it, many normal people are wary of coming in contact with them.

In spite of this social prejudice, the determination of cerebral palsy sufferers has placed them in almost every type of occupation. As a young high school student, Mick Joyce, a victim of cerebral palsy, was discouraged by those around him when he expressed an interest in going to college. He has since graduated from college, has his poetry published in a number of journals, and is presently compiling a catalogue of information relevant to the civil rights of the disabled. He has received a foundation grant to pursue this work.

Daniel A. Poling, a cerebral palsy victim, is the editor of a news magazine, *Polling,* published by the United Cerebral Palsy Foundation, devoted to issues of special importance to the disabled.

Many cerebral palsy victims are not as fortunate as these. They are the ones whose mental ability has been impaired or who are not able to gain enough control of their movements to allow them to be self-sustaining. But no matter how severe their limitations, the cerebral palsied are entitled to a life of dignity. They need not be institutionally warehoused. Every human being has a potential, and no matter how small that of the handicapped may appear in the eyes of the whole and healthy, he has the right to fulfill it.

Fortunately, today there are alternatives to being shut away for the cerebral palsied. There are workshops that provide both job training and employment opportunities for those unable to work under ordinary conditions. And there are new communal dwellings and residences for the cerebral palsied that offer a more homelike atmosphere within the community. Many cerebral palsy sufferers, formerly classified as "hopeless," have made great strides when given the opportunity to prove their abilities and to assume responsibility within the family and community. Their achievements are that much more significant, considering the obstacles they had to overcome.

Multiple Sclerosis

About a quarter-million Americans are afflicted with multiple sclerosis, and another 250,000 have related dis-

A normal game of hockey? That's right. But all the players here are deaf. *(Courtesy of the Office of Public Information, Pre-college Programs, Gallaudet College, Washington, D.C.)*

The deaf, like everyone else, enjoy participating in all sports, including soccer. (*Courtesy of the Office of Public Information, Pre-college Programs, Gallaudet College, Washington, D.C.*)

This young half-back running for a touchdown is deaf. *(Courtesy of the Office of Public Information, Pre-college Programs, Gallaudet College, Washington, D.C.)*

Kate Adams, the 1975 quadraplegic archery champion. *(Kay's Photo Service from United Cerebral Palsy Association)*

Disabled children visiting a "haunted house." *(Gordon Alexander from United Cerebral Palsy Association)*

His style may be a bit unorthodox, but that doesn't keep this discus thrower from achieving his goal. (*United Cerebral Palsy of Detroit*)

The batter appears to disagree with the umpire's call. *(United Cerebral Palsy Association)*

Fishing on a lazy summer afternoon. *(United Cerebral Palsy Association of Fairfield County, Inc.)*

eases. Multiple sclerosis attacks young adults usually between the ages of twenty and thirty-five. It is found most commonly in cold, damp climates, and occurs slightly more frequently in women than in men.

The disease attacks the fatty tissue, myelin, that sheathes the nerve fibers of the brain and spinal cord. This sheath ordinarily protects and insulates the nerve fibers. When attacked by multiple sclerosis, this sheath breaks down and is later replaced by scar, or sclerotic, tissue. These patches of sclerotic tissue can be found scattered throughout the nervous system, hence the name *multiple sclerosis*. This scarring of the protective myelin sheathing impairs the flow of nerve impulses along the fibers contained within; if the disease penetrates to the nerve fibers themselves, and scars them as well, nerve impulses will stop altogether.

The effects of the disease vary widely from case to case, depending upon the degree of damage to the myelin or nerve fibers. Symptoms ranging from mild numbness or tingling in the extremities, blurred vision, slurred speech, and faulty co-ordination, to the more severe loss of bladder or bowel control, complete or partial paralysis of legs and arms, blindness and deafness result from the interruption of nerve impulses from the brain.

Although the disease is progressive, i.e., its effects usually worsen with time, it follows no steady, predictable course. In only a small percentage of cases do the symptoms continue to worsen right from the start. In most cases, symptoms come and go in the beginning, sometimes disappearing completely. This disappearance is called a "remission," and the reoccurrence of an old symptom or the appearance of a new one is called a "relapse." Periods of remission can continue for years, before a relapse occurs. In some cases, remission is permanent. In still others, a symptom or group of symptoms may appear suddenly and persist without either improvement or progression. In these instances the person's condition remains stable throughout his life.

The cause of multiple sclerosis is unknown, although the findings of much current research seem to indicate that multiple sclerosis is quite likely brought on by an unknown slow-acting virus or autoimmunity, in which the body develops an allergic reaction to its own tissues. Since multiple sclerosis tends to occur primarily in the temperate zone, it is widely held that the environment plays some part in its development. The possibility that certain individuals may have a genetic predisposition to multiple sclerosis is also being explored. At the present time there is no specific treatment for multiple sclerosis, although some symptoms can be alleviated through drugs or physiotherapy.

Contrary to popular belief, the person who has been diagnosed as having multiple sclerosis does not necessarily face a lifetime of gradual degeneration, confined to a wheel chair grimly awaiting death. Many are able to carry on with normal or near-normal activity despite their symptoms or periods of incapacity.

According to one expert: "Multiple sclerosis is greatly variable in its manifestations in different individuals suffering from this disorder. This lack of uniformity makes it imperative that each person with the disease be evaluated individually for purposes of employment and rehabilitation. It has been increasingly apparent in recent years that the disease is considerably less devastating *on the average* than it was formerly believed."[†]

[†] *Facts for Employers About Multiple Sclerosis,* National Multiple Sclerosis Society, pamphlet, quoting C. A. D'Alonzo, M.D., Medical Director of E. I. Du Pont De Nemours & Co., Inc., 1972.

Many have been able to make excellent adjustments to their disability and continue their work as lawyers, teachers, doctors, musicians, secretaries, housewives, bankers, executives, bookkeepers, mail carriers, coal miners and so on. But like so many others who suffer from disabling disorders, the multiple sclerosis victim may have difficulty securing or holding a job once his condition is made known.

In some instances the mere mention of multiple sclerosis will bring immediate rejection. This is because most people are misinformed as to the varying severity of the condition and are unaware that many multiple sclerosis sufferers can be virtually symptom free throughout much of their adult lives, or have symptoms so mild or controllable that they need not interfere with their work.

Because this fear of multiple sclerosis is so widespread, many physicians are reluctant to tell their patients that they have the disease, even when they are sure of the diagnosis. For psychological, economic and social reasons, they want to protect their patients from their own as well as society's adverse reactions. It can be quite devastating for someone to discover he has multiple sclerosis, if he himself holds a vague, misinformed vision of fate-worse-than-death consequences.

But instead of withholding this vital information from their patients, doctors should help them to a better understanding of their condition. The knowledge that multiple sclerosis need not be as debilitating as was once feared, along with a positive attitude about the future, is perhaps the best medicine available to the multiple sclerosis sufferer. The patient who is knowledgeable about his own condition, is then able to educate those around him through his actions. Public enlightenment regarding the facts about multiple sclerosis can only benefit victim and non-victim alike.

Muscular Dystrophy

The term muscular dystrophy, or more accurately, dystrophies, refers to a group of chronic disorders characterized by the progressive degeneration of muscle tissue. The age of onset, rate of progression, and initial muscle group affected vary according to the type of dystrophy.

In its most common forms, early signs of dystrophy are usually very slight and are often ignored; but as the muscles deteriorate, the individual becomes progressively weaker. In the final stages of the disease, the individual is no longer able to do anything for himself. He has no strength and is almost defenseless against infections. Death usually results from respiratory or heart failure.

There are approximately 250,000 Americans who suffer from some form of muscular dystrophy, two thirds of whom are children between the ages of three and fifteen. It is believed that the major types of dystrophy are hereditary in origin, and sex-linked (in most cases women are the carriers and men are the receivers of the affected gene) but it is not known in precisely what way the genetic defect triggers the muscular deterioration. There is no effective treatment for any of the dystrophies, although some symptoms can be relieved through drug and physical therapy, and certain orthopedic devices may prove helpful at different stages in its progression.

The prognosis for the severely dystrophied child is generally a slow decline that leads to an early death and thus he is in need of particularly sensitive handling and treatment. Because the intelligence of the dystrophic child is ordinarily unaffected by his condition, he will most likely be quite capable of understanding the implications of the fatal nature of his condition. He must be given the emotional support he needs in order to cope with the difficult situation, and to live the fullest possible life for as long as he is able. He must be allowed to do whatever he can for himself, and encouraged to maintain a positive attitude throughout.

"The child must and can be prepared for the future, whatever this may hold. If the progress of the disease should in the future be further retarded or curtailed, it would be unfortunate if the dystrophic population were unprepared to meet the demands of the adult life that would become theirs. At the moment, of course, the problem is concerned with adjustment to incapacitating and fatal illness."‡

Mental Retardation

The term "mental retardation" refers to a condition of limited intellectual functioning, characterized by abnormally slow personal development. The mental age and abilities of the retarded person always lag behind those of his peers, and further intellectual growth is ordinarily halted after he reaches a certain level. He will remain at that developmental plateau for the rest of his life.

For the purposes of education, the more than 6 million Americans who are mentally retarded are usually divided

‡ Sherwin, Albert C., M.D., *Psychological and Emotional Aspects of Muscular Dystrophy*, New York: M.D.A. of America.

into three classifications according to their capabilities. The *educable*, or the mildly retarded, are able to do some academic work, such as reading and writing, and can be trained to be self-supporting and relatively independent. The *trainable*, or the severely retarded, will not profit from academic education, but they can learn to take care of their personal needs and do some work, although they will always need a protective and supportive environment. The *dependent* or profoundly retarded will be unable to care for themselves adequately and will remain in need of continuous assistance throughout their lives.

Profound retardation is usually quite noticeable during infancy. It is the result of extensive brain damage or malformation, and it often occurs in company with other neurological disorders, most commonly cerebral palsy and epilepsy. Some of the more striking but rare types of mental retardation include: *Down's syndrome*, more commonly known as mongoloidism because of the peculiar facial characteristics associated with it, is caused by the presence of an extra chromosome in the child's genetic make-up; *cretinism*, a thyroid gland malfunction that can be treated with some success if detected early enough; *phenylketonuria* (PKU), a liver dysfunction that allows toxic substances to affect the brain; and *hydrocephaly*, or water on the brain.

Mild retardation is much more widespread than the severe or profound forms, and unlike the others is most often not the result of neurological abnormality. The problem of the "slow learner" as the mildly retarded child is often called, is usually rooted in the environment. Malnutrition, disease and cultural deprivation are some of the more prominent contributing factors.

NEUROLOGICAL DYSFUNCTIONS 69

The key feature of the retarded child's development is his slowness. He is slow to develop in all areas—the physical and social as well as the intellectual. As an infant, he may not cry very much and be mistakenly thought of as a "good baby." This is not the case, however. He is just unable to express his basic needs as readily as the normal baby. He will show less awareness of his surroundings, less curiosity, and will appear content to just lie in his crib, staring vacantly into space.

As he grows older, the retarded child will display difficulty in fine motor co-ordination, such as in tying his shoelaces, batting a ball, buttoning his coat, writing, etc. He will be restless and unable to concentrate for long periods, and he will have trouble adapting his behavior patterns to suit acceptable social requirements. His life will be more difficult than the normal child's, and he is likely to experience more failures. By the time he reaches school age, he may be so afraid of failure he will be reluctant to try anything new.

The older he gets and the wider the gap grows between his peers and himself the more aware of his own shortcomings he becomes. He cannot keep up with his peers, as their taunts, jeers and exclusion from their activities constantly remind him. His fears and their rejection may cause him to feel isolated and to become withdrawn. Loneliness and isolation are ever-present dangers. Lack of companionship and non-acceptance by other children are among the greatest problems the retarded child will face.

Many parents are reluctant to believe their child is retarded and ascribe his lagging abilities to laziness. They may pressure him to work harder and do better. His inability to please his parents adds to his growing list of frustrations.

By the time he reaches adolescence, the retarded child may begin to express strong fears of "growing up," because he can't see any future for himself, or just where he fits in the normal world. This is partly due to a limitation in foresight and an inability to project himself into situations he hasn't yet experienced, that is a part of his disability.

But it is also due to circumstances quite outside himself, to the very real lack of provision made for him by society. Adolescence is a trying time for every teen-ager who feels suspended in the limbo that exists between childhood and adulthood. Think of how much more trying it is for the retarded teen-ager, with the mental age of a nine-year-old, who can sense that the rewards of adulthood—responsibility, freedom, independence—are not awaiting him after he passes through the trial of adolescence.

There is no cure for the condition known as mental retardation, but that does not mean that the mentally retarded child does not have a potential and that his potential, no matter how small, should not be developed. He has the same right to a sense of dignity in fulfillment as the rest of us have, and every effort should be made to encourage him in his struggle to fill his cup of achievement to the brim. He should not be made to feel guilty about something he has no control over, and he should not be made to feel worthless because he can't throw a baseball as well as his brother, or takes twenty minutes to tie his shoes, or can't do his multiplication tables. He must be allowed to build on his strengths, not be condemned because of his weaknesses.

Unfortunately, the tide of history is weighted against

the chances of the retarded for personal, albeit limited, achievement. In ancient times the mentally retarded were ridiculed, made the butt of jokes and traditionally cast out of polite society. The characterization of the "village idiot" and the "fool" are familiar to us all. But it is in just this role of "fool" that history has perhaps shown a subtle irony with regard to the retarded.

The term fool originally meant a kind of entertainer, and the fool at court was usually one of the king's most loyal and trusted servants. It was at times believed that the disconnected ramblings of the fool were the words of the gods.

The fool was an awe-inspiring figure whose reason had ceased to function normally, because he was possessed by a spirit, who endowed him with supernatural powers, most especially the ability to look into the future. With such power it is no wonder that the fool often became the king's number one advisor. And the fool who took advantage of his position, as many did, was certainly no fool in the modern sense of the word. Such fortunate fools were few and far between, however, and most mentally deficient individuals were considered "offspring of the evil one" (Martin Luther), were thrown in prisons or dungeons and scourged for "their own good" (the middle ages), or sacrificed to the gods (in ancient times—but only because they were considered somehow the peculiar property of the gods; the French still call the mentally disabled, *les enfants de bon Dieu*, the children of God).

As more humane treatment for those who were "different" began to be adopted throughout the Western world, hospitals and asylums were set up to house them; but because of an inability to discriminate among the causes of differences, the mentally retarded were often confined with the insane. After the "Age of Enlightenment," institutions were created specifically for the care of the mentally retarded, but these were purely custodial with no real treatment involved.

Today there is a new emphasis on the education, training and "rehabilitation" of the mentally retarded. Special education facilities, where the retarded child is allowed to learn at his own rate, are helping the retarded realize their full potential. Those that are able to be self-supporting are encouraged to work and assimilate themselves into the community. It has been found that the mentally retarded make good factory workers because they are not as easily bored by the routine work as other workers. For them it is a challenge and responsibility.

Other occupations suitable for the retarded include service station attendant, farmworker, file clerk, nurse's aid, receptionist, bus boy, construction worker and so on.

Those retarded persons who are not able to manage on their own have been able to work well in the sheltered workshop situation. The sheltered workshop provides an actual occupational setting for the retarded person similar in most respects to the usual industrial setting, but without competition. Each worker proceeds at his own pace on a variety of jobs, usually subcontracted from industry, ranging from simple packaging to reasonably complicated collation and assembly.

Even the most profoundly retarded child can be infused with a sense of worth and the pride of achievement when given the opportunity to develop to the limits of his potential. Often these limits extend far beyond initial expectations. Most people of normal intelligence would be amazed at what a severely or profoundly retarded child is capable of when provided with an atmosphere of love, understanding and encouragement.

Programs, like the Special Olympics, sponsored by the Joseph P. Kennedy, Jr., Foundation, provide just such an atmosphere. In the words of Eunice Kennedy Shriver, Special Olympics is ". . . a comprehensive year-round program of training, recreation and sports competition in almost every type of athletic event and physical skill." The result of this and other programs, according to Mrs. Shriver, is that mentally retarded children ". . . are becoming *healthy*. By this I don't simply mean physical fitness. These young people are experiencing health in other significant dimensions. Because of new skills and accomplishments, they have a higher regard for themselves. Because their parents, brothers and sisters see them achieving results, they are developing healthy family relationships. Because classmates see them achieving success, there is a healthier acceptance in school and throughout the community."

What the Special Olympics proves is that retarded children are as capable of growth and development as anyone and should be allowed the right to live in an atmosphere that fosters their growth. And that atmosphere is not found in an institution that merely maintains the individual. It is to be found only in the mainstream of society, not apart from it.

Mrs. Shriver sums up the plight of the retarded in America today when she writes:

> We still have far to go. Many who do not know the retarded don't consider them fully human. They're usually the first to be set apart, . . . the first to be experimented upon,

the first to be denied basic rights and privileges. The greatest protection the retarded have is familiarity and awareness. We must recognize their great strengths as human beings. They show courage and skill and they are loyal devoted friends. When they are treated as equals, they are hard working and productive. Most of the mentally retarded . . . are capable of independent, constructive citizenship.

Being Crippled

Hundreds of children and adults in this country are afflicted every year with what are known as orthopedic, crippling or musculoskeletal defects. "Birth defects" or "congenital defects" are terms used widely to encompass all crippling defects that occur as a result of damage to the infant in the uterus or some developmental failure that occurs before birth. Some of the more obvious birth defects include club feet, dislocated hips, missing limbs or joints, curvature of the spine, spina bifida, i.e., an opening in the spinal cord that if not corrected surgically can cut off feeling in the lower extremities, and dwarfism.

After birth, diseases such as polio, rheumatoid arthritis (inflammation of the joints), and osteomyelitis (bone disease), conditions like infantile hemoplegia (a brain hemorrhage called a stroke in adults), or accidents can all result in orthopedic crippling of varying degree. Congenitally crippling defects and those caused by accident are usually stable, that is, they do not worsen with time, and can often be treated with surgery, physiotherapy or aids such as braces. Where there is limb loss a prosthesis (artificial limb) can be used in its place. In the case of crippling diseases, such as arthritis, drug therapy may be called for to halt the progressive degeneration of the affected parts of the body, in combination with physiotherapy to restore use of areas already damaged.

The child who is orthopedically crippled may suffer a great deal of emotional stress because his defect is so readily visible to those around him. He may become extremely self-conscious and fearful of mingling with other children.

In her children's fairy tale, *The Little Lame Prince*, Dinah Craik aptly illustrates the reactions of a little boy as he comes to the realization that his legs will not permit him to run and play like the other children he sees. "You're no good to me," the little prince says, "patting" his useless legs mournfully. "You never will be any good to me. I wonder why I had you at all. I wonder why I was born at all, since I was not to grow up like other boys."

Another children's book, *Don't Feel Sorry for Paul* by Bernard Wolf, tells the true story of young Paul Jockimo, the victim of crippling birth defects that left him with improperly formed feet, just two fingers on his left arm, and only a stump (no hand or fingers) at the end of his right arm. He wears an arm prosthesis equipped with a movable two-pronged steel hook, that he is able to manipulate almost as effectively as a real hand. He has learned to function quite well with his prosthesis, but when he first started going to school, some of his classmates made fun of him, calling him "Captain Hook." Paul would try to ignore them. Sometimes the other boys would try to catch him off guard. "They thought he couldn't defend himself. When Paul angrily whirled around and raised his hook in a threatening manner, they ran away."

Paul's aggressive behavior and the fictional Prince's withdrawal are both common reactions of children so afflicted. Some fight back when cruelly confronted with the fact of their difference, while others run away and hide. Only a great deal of love and understanding can correct these anti-social tendencies and help the child to make the difficult but necessary adjustment to his disability.

The child afflicted with an orthopedic disability may have the added emotional strain of being subjected to long-term treatment that can include numerous operations, prolonged drug therapy, or physiotherapy, often with no real assurance of their ultimate outcome. With such constant attention to the child's disability, family and doctors run the risk of ignoring his other very real needs. Treatment may keep him away from school and the contact of other children for long periods of time, which may retard his social, educational and emotional growth.

Special effort should be made to care for the *total* child and to avoid concentrating on just his physical needs at the expense of his emotional ones. Paul Jockimo's family and friends were able to avoid these pitfalls in caring for him, and his story has a happy ending. Because of their encouragement Paul is able to enjoy horseback riding, playing football and riding his bicycle. He's made a healthy adjustment to his disability and he has been accepted by his peers, although he might still be asked what happened to his arm or how his "hook thing" works. Paul tells them that he was born the way he is, and shows them how his own prosthesis works. This usually satisfies their curiosity.

Unfortunately, not all orthopedically crippled children are allowed to make the good adjustment Paul has. Because of the ordinarily extreme visibility of their disability, the lame, the crippled, the deformed, have been particularly vulnerable to social disapproval. The ancient Greeks and Spartans left their deformed children to die of exposure or neglect, with the notable exceptions of Aesop, the renowned storyteller, and Pittakos, a king of Athens, both of whom were crippled.

In the middle ages orthopedic cripples were popular as entertainers at court. Dwarfs fetched a particularly high price as novelty slaves, and there are stories of normal children being bound so that their growth would be stunted, in order that they might be sold as dwarfs. The same economic considerations prevailed at the lower end of the social scale as well; impoverished parents often mutilated their own children, because a deformed beggar always drew more sympathy, which usually meant more money. William Shakespeare reflects the rampant prejudice against cripples in his day in his plays, most notably in the character of Caliban in *The Tempest*.

Many men have risen above the general hostility toward the orthopedically disabled, to make their mark on history. Lord Byron, the flamboyant English poet, renowned for his physical beauty and romantic exploits as much as for his poetry, had a congenitally clubbed foot. Peter Stuyvesant, the American colonial leader, was a leg amputee, who got around with the help of a wooden leg. Franklin D. Roosevelt suffered from crippling polio, but that didn't stop him from being the only President of the United States to be elected to four consecutive terms of office. Harold Russell, perhaps best known for his Academy Award-winning portrayal of Homer Parrish, the young sailor who returns home from World War II after having lost both his hands, in the film classic, *The Best Years of Our Lives*, serves as the chairman of the President's Committee on Employment of the Handicapped. The handless detective, Jay J. Armes, who is equipped with hooked prostheses, has captured the imagination of the country with his daring exploits.

Their highly visible differences make the orthopedically crippled especially vulnerable to the prejudices of the normal who can make their lives quite difficult. They should remember the words of a young woman confined to a wheel chair for thirty years who said:

> Believe me, I don't enjoy looking at myself in the mirror. It's a painful feeling but, nevertheless, it's something I can work through and accept.
>
> It's important not to reject your body. Ultimately, I think a good adjustment comes when you can accept the ugly with the not so ugly, or the ugly with the beautiful. If you have a deformed leg, it's still you.
>
> My body, fortunately, does not define my whole being. I believe in self-actualization—that is, no matter what kind of limitations a person may have, there's no real reason why he or she shouldn't engage in relationships characteristic of life itself.*

* Mary Jane Tesch, quoted in "The Handicapped Consumer-Professional Speaks," by Joy Schlaben Lewis, *Polling*, November 1974, Vol. 1, No. 2; article reprinted from *The Journal of Rehabilitation*, March–April, 1974.

A Word About Multihandicaps

Disabilities often occur in combinations, and those who are afflicted with more than one physical defect are said to possess a multiple handicap. It is not uncommon for a cerebral palsied child to suffer also from impaired vision and/or hearing. Mental retardation often occurs together with other physical defects. It would seem that those so extremely disabled would not be able to function at all in normal society, would need constant care, and would be better off in an institution. This may be true in some cases, but it is also true that each individual, no matter how severely limited his life choices may be, has the right to live as full and complete a life as he is able. He should be encouraged to reach and grow as far as he can even within the confines of an institution.

Joseph Deacon, a severely palsied and spastic Englishman who had trouble speaking and making himself understood, was wrongly classified as mentally retarded throughout most of his early life. (Intelligence is often underestimated in the case of the multiple handicapped due to the obvious difficulties involved in measuring it.) He had spent nearly all of his adult life in an institution, when, with the aid of a team of friends there, he wrote his autobiography. He painstakingly dictated the words to the one friend who could understand his faulty speech, and the friend, in turn, translated what he said to another who was able to write. Mr. Deacon then dictated the written manuscript, letter by letter, via his interpreter, to yet another who was able to type. The result, *Tongue Tied*, took over a year to produce, but no one who is familiar with his story could possibly argue that the reward was not well worth the effort.

Everyone is familiar with the dramatic story of the life of Helen Keller who was blind and deaf from infancy. She was able to overcome one of the most severe combinations of disabilities, and go on to lead a life that would be considered remarkable by any standard.

So the next time you're tempted to think of a severely handicapped individual as a "hopeless case," think about the achievements of Joseph Deacon, Helen Keller and the countless others even less fortunate than they who are overcoming similar hurdles every day of their lives.

Part III

Future Outlook

... It is no longer acceptable for anyone in placing a prop under [a] body to place a ceiling over his potential achievements.

Earl Schenck Miers

What Next for the Disabled?

As we have seen over and over again, the attitudes and prejudices of society are at least equally as devastating to the handicapped as are their actual physical limitations. It is society's reaction to the disability that makes or breaks the individual's chances of leading a "normal" life. It is society that makes the rules, and we either conform or risk being ostracized because of our differences.

Throughout history, normal society has adopted a number of different and often conflicting poses toward the disabled. At times the disabled have been merely ignored as being beneath the dignity of recognition; at others they have been dealt with more harshly: they have been cruelly cast out, driven from the fold with vengeance; they have been ridiculed and laughed at as objects fit only for our amusement; they have even been honored and revered above other men; and most recently they have been locked away in institutions for their "own good." In all these varied social dispositions, whether cruel or humane, there has been one uniting thread, and that is the prevailing policy of exclusion, of removal of the deviant from normal social interaction.

We have also seen that there is absolutely no basis in fact for these primarily negative social reactions toward the disabled. There is no real physical necessity for their enforced isolation. They cannot contaminate or harm us with their presence. They can pose no real threat to us. In fact, society has actually done itself a disservice by its policy of exclusion, because it has lost a tremendous human resource in the process. Society only stands to benefit from the acceptance of its disabled members because whenever they have had the still all too rare opportunity to participate fully in the social mainstream, they have proven themselves more than capable. In the previous sections we have read of many disabled individuals who have lead active, productive lives. Unfortunately, these success stories remain the exception rather than the rule, but they do represent the vanguard of a growing movement to integrate the disabled into the social mainstream.

This movement represents the latest stage in the historical development of society's treatment of the disabled. Civilization has gone through several stages to reach this level of social awareness—through the primitive banishment or sentence of death by neglect of the physically deviant; to the imprisonment of those who were physically different; to their indiscriminate hospitalization with no regard as to the kinds, causes or treatment of their physical problems; to the purely institutional, custodial care for the disabled; to the present stage which emphasizes the rehabilitation and social integration of the disabled.

Perhaps the next stage will bring discoveries of new ways to cure and prevent disabilities; research goes on constantly toward those ends. In the meantime we must concentrate our efforts on what we can do for the disabled right now, and that is to assimilate them into the social mainstream as full participants, and educate those localities that continue to lag behind in less-enlightened stages of

Campers enjoy a visit with Ronald McDonald. *(B & L Photographers from United Cerebral Palsy Association)*

Scouting is for everyone. *(United Cerebral Palsy Association of Utica)*

A disabled boy enjoys a dip in the pool with a little help from a friend. *(Minneapolis Tribune)*

A camper appraises his catch. (*Muscular Dystrophy Associations*)

A group of young people with muscular dystrophy enjoying archery at summer camp. *(Muscular Dystrophy Associations)*

Harold Russell, a double amputee, is chairman of the President's Committee on Employment of the Handicapped. *(President's Committee on Employment of the Handicapped)*

Lord Byron, the great English poet, who had a clubfoot.
(Painting by Thomas Phillips)

A group of disabled persons caused a traffic jam when they demonstrated in front of the office of the governor of New York in 1974. The disabled have begun adopting the tactics of other minority groups in their struggle for their basic rights. *(Photograph by The New York Times)*

regard for the disabled, to a more progressive way of dealing with them.

And there is much that needs to be done, given that: "One out of every eleven Americans is disabled. Fifty-two per cent have incomes of less that $2,000 a year. Sixty per cent of the disabled adults never finished high school. The lowest official poverty level—the poorest of the poor—has a proportion of handicapped people twice as high as the non-disabled population."† Disabled Americans, with the help of their able-bodied supporters, have finally begun to organize themselves for the purpose of redressing the imbalances just quoted. They are demanding their rights to full citizenship, as guaranteed in the Constitution.

These rights include equal education, fair housing, equal employment opportunity, and the removal of all environmental, psychological and communication barriers to their human and civil rights. The government, the courts, and the people of this country are at long last taking a serious look at the plight of the disabled and doing what needs to be done to improve their status in our society.

The movement for a "barrier-free" environment has been one of the more successful efforts launched by this new coalition of the disabled. One of the biggest and most immediate problems confronting the physically disabled today is their lack of mobility. Things that the rest of us take for granted like curbs, stairs, revolving doors, escalators, narrow doorways are all potential obstacles to the free movement of the disabled. Try maneuvering around your home or neighborhood in a wheel chair for a day, and you'll soon understand what is at stake.

In response to this issue the United States Congress

† *Crusader*, United Cerebral Palsy, New York, Spring 1975, p. 2.

enacted the 1968 Architectural Barriers Act which requires that ". . . any building constructed in whole or in part with federal funds must be accessible to and usable by the handicapped." The 1973 Rehabilitation Act supported the 1968 legislation with the establishment of the Architectural Barriers Compliance Board, which has the power to ". . . conduct investigations, hold public hearings and issue such orders as it deems necessary to insure compliance." Forty-nine out of the fifty states have laws including the same accessibility conditions for state-financed buildings. Pressure is being brought to bear upon private construction concerns to make their buildings accessible, and attention is being focused on the special problems inherent in most standard transportation facilities.

Although these laws are not yet being adequately enforced, the outlook for a barrier-free environment is improving every day. In 1977 Secretary of Health, Education and Welfare Joseph Califano signed measures providing for stricter enforcement. People are gradually coming to accept the fact that the handicapped have the right to "total freedom of choice as to where they wish to work, play, study, and live; and that no man-made [barrier] must be allowed to prevent this."‡

Barrier freedom is not only limited to architecture, but includes a wide variety of things the normal take for granted.

Most products—door handles, water fountains, television and appliance controls, even packaging—are based on criteria developed for so-called "normal" groups. This design

‡ Stephen A. Klimet, quoted from his booklet, *Into the Mainstream: A Syllabus for a Barrier-Free Environment*, printed by the A.I.A., in the *Easter Seal Communicator*, Chicago, June 1975.

discrimination can be easily eliminated through the development of standards for production that would accommodate the disabled. The end result would be a far more universal product, that would benefit everyone, normal and disabled alike.

Another issue of paramount importance to the disabled is education. A 1974 Department of Health, Education and Welfare report on services for the disabled states that ". . . whether a child receives special educational assistance, and the amount of that assistance, depend unmistakably and strongly on where his parents live." In other words, some states are not providing disabled children adequate public education, a clear violation of their constitutional rights.

It has been the custom in this country to set up separate schools for the physically disabled, but these schools have been few and far between and largely inaccessible to the majority of those who need them. In addition, the policy of separate school facilities is in itself deleterious to the disabled child. When it becomes time to leave the protective environment of the "special school," the disabled individual may not be prepared to deal with the real world. If he has always been separated throughout his school life into an artificial stream, he may lack the capacity to understand or to work with others of differing ability. The disabled child must be assimilated as much as possible into the mainstream of society right from the start, not separated or segregated, and that means he should attend school along with everyone else. A disability does not necessarily imply an impairment or loss of learning ability—even the most severely disabled child is able to *learn* some things— but only an inability to obtain adequate information via an impaired receptor, i.e., eyes, ears etc.

Instead of separating the child because of his weaknesses, we should educate him according to his strengths. In a number of cases over the years, the Supreme Court has reaffirmed the right of the disabled child to the "least restricted alternative" in education. This means that the disabled child cannot be removed from a public school without good cause and due process of the law. The intent of the court is clear: Public schools have the obligation to serve all students regardless of their disabilities.

Eunice Shriver's comments about the effects of the court rulings on the mentally retarded are applicable to all disabled children.

> The public schools of America are opening up to the mentally retarded—because the courts are at last giving retarded boys and girls their rights to an equal education. This intermingling of the retarded in the educational mainstream is considered the best way of "normalizing" them and integrating them into society. As children come to know them as friends and schoolmates, they will recognize that the similarities outweigh the differences between them.

Finding adequate employment continues to present a major problem for a great number of disabled persons. Success in the workplace has always been the measure of a successful human being in America. Pride in a job well done and the recognition of one's peers is one of the greatest sources of ego fulfillment known in the Western world. Those who are not gainfully employed are looked down upon as irresponsible shirkers or helpless incompetents. The majority of the disabled who are unemployed or underemployed fit neither of these categories. They also seek the gratification of a rewarding occupation.

One mentally retarded man summed up the plight of all the disabled trying to find work when he said:

> When you been out of work so long and can't seem to get no job you really worry: Is there something wrong with me or something? A man's got a right to work. Besides, you're better off when you're doing something. It puts your mind at ease, makes you feel like you're as good as everybody else.

Some widespread myths among employers regarding the employment of the disabled are that costly adjustments in the work area will have to be made to accommodate them, insurance rates and accident records will soar, absenteeism and worker turnover rates among the disabled will be excessive. Surveys of disabled workers in industry have shown, however, that quite the opposite is true. Disabled workers tend to have even better work records than the non-disabled, and they usually require no special work arrangements.

According to Jane B. Sprain, vice-president of the United States Civil Service Commission:

> The handicapped person who is properly trained and job matched is usually dependable and reliable, showing up on the job every day. He is more safety conscious, with an almost zero accident rate. Once placed, he doesn't jump from job to job, so he costs the company less in on-the-job training. He is so grateful for a job that he out-produces the able-bodied in quantity and quality. What is more, he raises the morale of his workmates, which helps improve everyone's production.

The glowing record of the disabled employee gives the lie to all the traditional reasons for denying him employment, and the law supports his right to work.

Housing of the disabled plays an important part in their integration into the community, for as long as they are isolated in institutions, they will never be a part of the social mainstream. The trend today is toward smaller residential dwellings for groups of the disabled, such as the mentally retarded and severely cerebral palsied, that provide the special attention and care that might be needed along with easy access to the community at large.

The increased visibility of the disabled within the heart of the community and the expanded opportunity for social interaction cannot help but break down the barriers between the "normal" and the disabled. It is this kind of familiarity, and first-hand experience, that is the best antidote to the irrational fears and prejudices of the non-disabled toward the disabled. The more the non-disabled actually witness the disabled functioning in their world, in their neighborhood, the more they will grow to accept them as their social equals.

In the community, at school, at work or play, provision must be made to include everyone in every activity of our society. We can no longer continue our policy of exclusion based on arbitrary physical and mental standards if we expect to survive as a functioning, healthy social unit. Human potential is our country's most valuable natural resource, and we cannot afford to proceed indefinitely with its indiscriminate waste. There must be a place for every man no matter what his strengths or weaknesses.

The following story is an illustration of one society's very natural way of integrating its disabled members. An anthropologist was studying the life style of a certain African tribe. One morning he watched as the people in a particular village prepared to start the day. He caught sight of a young man leading an elderly, obviously blind man

WHAT NEXT FOR THE DISABLED? 93

across the compound. The young man seemed to be having some difficulty negotiating their way. When the anthropologist asked his guide about the odd pair, he was told that the blind man was one of the village elders, and, as such, greatly revered for his wisdom and his position on the tribal council. Although the younger man was apparently retarded, and thus unable to engage in the normal pursuits of his peers, such as hunting and farming, he was still able to participate as a functioning member of his social unit. His eyes and legs were intact, and he could guide the blind elder about the village.

Even in this "primitive" society, each person has been allowed to serve according to his ability, not excluded because of his weakness. The old man is still respected for his wisdom although he has lost his vision, and the retarded boy is made useful because he still has two good eyes. The way in which this society provides for its disabled members appears so simple, so logical, yet it is this kind of simple logic that still eludes many of us in our supposedly "advanced" society.

The society that is flexible, that can accept differences, is a healthy one. The society that can absorb and use every one of its members, whether it be "primitive" or "advanced," is a society that will survive and grow. The society that gives all men the chance to prove their worth, to contribute, to fulfill their potential, is ultimately the successful one. We can build that society in this country, but only if our disabled brothers and sisters are allowed to participate in its construction. Together we can build a sound social structure, that will stand proudly supported by the combined effort, strength and achievement of all its citizens.

A normal person to a disabled one: "Affliction does so color life."

The disabled person's response: "Yes, and I propose to choose the color!"

Glossary

ADJUSTMENT. Personal adaptation to and acceptance of something that is new or unusual. A person who has come to accept the limitations of his physical disability and continue to lead a useful life is said to have made a good adjustment to his condition.

ADVENTITIOUS. A physical condition that is not present at birth, but one that results from disease or accident occurring any time after birth.

BLINDISMS. Repeated self-stimulating mannerisms characteristic of the blind, such as rocking, rubbing the eyes etc.

BRAILLE. A system of touch reading for the blind consisting of combinations of raised dots that correspond to letters of the alphabet developed by Louis Braille in 1824.

CHRONIC. Constant and continuous.

COMPENSATION. The increased development of an organ or receptor to counterbalance the loss in effectiveness of another. That is, the development of a particularly acute sense of hearing in the blind. Contrary to popular belief, compensation for the loss of one sense by the heightened sensitivity of another is not automatic and must be learned.

CONGENITAL. A physical condition existing at or from birth.

DEVIANT. That which differs from the prescribed norm.

DISABILITY/HANDICAP. "A *disability* is the condition of a physical or mental defect or impairment that a person is born with or that he acquires by accident, injury or disease.

"A *handicap* is the limitation that the person—or other people—feels the disability imposes on him to affect his doing what he needs or wants to do or his being what he wants to be.

"To have a *disability* is not necessarily to have a *handicap*. The disability becomes a handicap only when the effects of it hamper the filling of a specific task or role at a specific time and place." (*Rehabilitation Is* . . . [New York: National Easter Seal Society for Crippled Children, 1972], unpaged.)

DISCRIMINATION. Unfair treatment of others based on personal bias.

GENETIC. Pertaining to the transmission of biologically inherited characteristics from parent to child.

ORTHOPEDIC. Having to do with the bones, joints, spine and muscles used in movement.

PREJUDICE. An unfair and irrational judgment that has no basis in fact but is rooted in fear, hatred and ignorance.

PROGRESSIVE. A physical condition that deteriorates in successive stages over a period of time.

PROSTHESIS. An artificial replacement for a missing body part such as a leg or arm.

REHABILITATION. The restoration of the disabled individual to the fullest physical, psychological, social, vocational and economic independence possible.

REMISSION. A temporary or permanent relief from a physical condition or its symptoms.

RELAPSE. The reoccurrence of a condition or symptoms that had previously been relieved, or the onset of new ones.

RETARDATION. Abnormally slow physical or mental development resulting from any one of a great variety of physical, emotional or social causes.

SOCIETY. A group of people, usually having geographical boundaries, who share certain characteristics such as language, culture, attitudes, beliefs, etc.

THERAPY. The treatment of disease or bodily disorder or injury with drugs, exercise etc.

TREATMENT. Therapeutic measures designed to cure or alleviate abnormal symptoms.

VERBALISM. The meaningless manipulation of words.

Bibliography

BOOKS

Ayrault, Evelyn West. *Helping the Handicapped Teenager Mature.* New York: Association Press, 1971.

Blodgett, Harriet E. *Mentally Retarded Children.* Minneapolis: University of Minnesota Press, 1971.

Bowley, Agatha H. *The Young Handicapped Child.* Edinburgh: E & S Livingstone, Ltd., 1957.

Burlingham, Dorothy. *Psychoanalytic Studies of the Sighted and the Blind.* New York: International Universities Press, 1972.

Connor, Leo E., ed. *Speech for the Deaf Child: Knowledge and Use.* Washington, D.C.: Alexander Graham Bell Association for the Deaf, 1971.

Dale, D. M. C. *Deaf Children at Home and at School.* London: University of London Press, 1967.

Dean, Russell J. N. *New Life for Millions: Rehabilitation for American Disabled.* New York: Hastings House Publishers, 1972.

Department of Health, Education and Welfare. *Improving Services for Handicapped Children.* Washington, D.C., 1974.

Dolch, William. *Helping Handicapped Children in School.* Champagne, Illinois: The Garrard Press, 1948.

Doman, Glenn. *What to Do About Your Brain-Injured Child.* Garden City: Doubleday & Company, Inc., 1974.

Eaton, Allen H. *Beauty for the Sighted and the Blind.* New York: St. Martin's Press, 1959.

Edgarton, Robert B. *The Cloak of Competence*. Berkeley: University of California Press, 1967.
Frampton, Merle E. and Rowell, Hugh Grant. *Education of the Handicapped*. Vol. 1. Yonkers, N.Y.: World Book Company, 1938.
French, Edward L. and Scott, J. Clifford. *How You Can Help Your Retarded Child*. Philadelphia: J. B. Lippincott Company, 1967.
French, Richard Slayton. *From Homer to Helen Keller, A Social and Educational Study of the Blind*. New York: American Foundation for the Blind, Inc., 1932.
Jenks, Rev. William F., C.S.S.R., ed. *The Atypical Child*. Washington, D.C.: The Catholic University of America Press, 1954.
Kershaw, John D. *Handicapped Children*. London: William Heinemann Medical Books, Ltd., 1966.
Kirman, Dr. Brian H. *The Mentally Handicapped Child*. New York: Taplinger Publishing Company, Inc., 1973.
Leland, Henry and Smith, Daniel E. *Mental Retardation: Present and Future Perspectives*. Worthington: Charles A. Jones Publishing Company, 1974.
Lowenfeld, Berthold. *Our Blind Children: Growing and Learning with Them*. Springfield, Ill.: Charles C. Thomas, 1971.
Lowenfeld, Berthold, ed. *The Visually Handicapped Child in School*. New York: John Day, 1973.
Lukens, Kathleen and Panter, Carol. *Thursday's Child Has Far to Go*. Englewood Cliffs: Prentice-Hall, Inc., 1969.
Mecham, Merlin J., et al., eds. *Communication Training in Childhood Brain Damage*. Springfield, Ill.: Charles C. Thomas, 1972.
Mykleburst, Helmer, ed. *Your Deaf Child: A Guide for Parents*. Springfield, Ill.: Charles C. Thomas, 1950.
Reusch, Joseph S., ed. *The Unusual Child*. New York: Philosophical Library, 1962.
Untermeyer, Louis. *Lives of the Poets*. New York: Simon and Schuster, 1959.
Weiner, Florence. *Help for the Handicapped Child*. New York: McGraw-Hill, 1973.

BIBLIOGRAPHY

Whitehouse, Elizabeth S. *There's Always More.* Valley Forge: The Judson Press, 1968.
Wright, David. *Deafness.* New York: Stein and Day, 1969.

PAMPHLETS, NEWSLETTERS, ETC.

Blindness

Facts About Blindness. New York: American Foundation for the Blind, Inc., 1975.
Growth and Development of the Partially Seeing Child. San Francisco: National Association for the Visually Handicapped, 1972.
Louis Braille. New York: American Foundation for the Blind, Inc., 1975.

Cerebral Palsy

Cerebral Palsy—Facts and Figures. New York: United Cerebral Palsy Associations, Inc., 1974.
Crusader. New York: United Cerebral Palsy Associations, Inc., Fall 1974.
Polling. Vol. 1, No. 2. New York: United Cerebral Palsy Associations, Inc., November 1974.
Seaver, Jacqueline. *Cerebral Palsy—More Hope than Ever.* New York: Public Affairs Pamphlets, 1967.
"SSU Graduate Once Judged 'Retarded' Get $17,582 Grant." Southwest Minnesota State College, News Release, September 4, 1975.
What Is Cerebral Palsy? New York: United Cerebral Palsy Associations, Inc., n.d.

Deafness

Annual Report. Year ended June 30, 1975. Silver Springs, N.Y.: National Association of the Deaf.
Deaf Adults. Silver Spring, Maryland: National Association of the Deaf.
Culton, Paul M., ed. *Operation Tripod, Toward Rehabilitation Involvement by Parents of the Deaf.* A Workshop sponsored

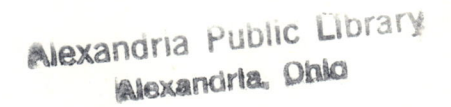

by the Department of Special and Rehabilitative Education. San Fernando Valley State College, 1971.
Sociological and Psychological Factors Associated with Hearing Loss. Silver Spring, Maryland: National Association of the Deaf.
Sounds or Silence? Washington, D.C.: Better Hearing Institute, 1976.
They Overcame Hearing Loss. Washington, D.C.: Better Hearing Institute, 1976.

Epilepsy

Answers to the Most Frequent Questions People Ask About Epilepsy. Washington, D.C.: Epilepsy Foundation of America, 1973.
Don't Be Afraid of the Child with Epilepsy. Washington, D.C.: Epilepsy Foundation of America, 1971.
Can Epilepsy Be Prevented? Washington, D.C.: Epilepsy Foundation of America, 1975.
Epilepsy: A Teenager's View. Washington, D.C.: Epilepsy Foundation of America, n.d.
Epilepsy School Alert. Washington, D.C.: Epilepsy Foundation of America, 1973.
History of the Epilepsy Movement in the United States. Washington, D.C.: Epilepsy Foundation of America, 1974.

Mental Retardation

Hello World! Arlington, Texas: National Association for Retarded Citizens, 1974.
MR-72, Islands of Excellence. Washington, D.C.: Report of the President's Committee on Mental Retardation, 1972.
MR-73, The Goal is Freedom. Washington, D.C.: Report of the President's Committee on Mental Retardation, 1973.
The AHRC Chronicle. New York: The Association for the Help of Retarded Children, June 1975.
The Right to Choose. Arlington, Texas: National Association for Retarded Citizens, 1973.

Tizard, J. *A Fresh Look at Retarded Children*. Arlington, Texas: National Association for Retarded Citizens, 1974.

Multiple Sclerosis

De Jong, Russel, M.D. *The Enemy of Young Adults*. New York: National Multiple Sclerosis Society, 1975.
Facts for Employers About Multiple Sclerosis. New York: National Multiple Sclerosis Society, 1972.
People at Work: Fifty Profiles of Men and Women with Multiple Sclerosis. New York: National Multiple Sclerosis Society and the President's Committee on Employment of the Handicapped.
1976 Fact Sheet on Multiple Sclerosis. New York: National Multiple Sclerosis Society, 1976.

Muscular Dystrophy

Around the Clock Aids for the Child with Muscular Dystrophy. New York: Muscular Dystrophy Associations of America, Inc., 1975.
Muscular Dystrophy Fact Sheet. New York: Muscular Dystrophy Associations of America, Inc.
Sherwin, Albert C. *Psychological and Emotional Aspects of Muscular Dystrophy*. New York: Muscular Dystrophy Associations of America, Inc.

General

Clutterbuck, David, assoc. ed. "Helping the Disabled Pay Their Way," *International Management*, June 1975. Reprint by the President's Committee on Employment of the Handicapped by Special Permission.
The Easter Seal Communicator. Chicago: National Easter Seal Society, June 1975.

ARTICLES

Brain Injury

"Disorder Infectious?" Indianapolis *Star*, March 3, 1976, p.6.
Flaste, Richard. "Parents of the Retarded Should Know the

Facts but too Often Don't," New York *Times.*
"Mary Ellen Is a Special Child," *Maine Sunday Telegram,* March 2, 1975, p. 4C.
Shriver, Eunice K. "Physical Education: Shortest Road to Success for the Handicapped," *Science and Children,* March 1976, pp. 24–26.

Blindness

Omwake, Eveline B. and Solnit, Albert J., M.D. *It Isn't Fair: The Treatment of a Blind Child.* New Haven: Child Study Center, Yale University, pp. 352–404.
"Blind Judge Is Sworn In by State Supreme Court," New York *Times,* December 13, 1975, p. 1.

Deafness

"Deaf Actors Speak with Bodies," Indianapolis *Star,* August 8, 1975.
Funke, Phyllis. "Deaf Mimes Set to Open Long Island Shows Wednesday," New York *Times,* August 3, 1975.
"Deafness—The Silent Epidemic," *Reader's Digest,* March 1974.
"Doctor I Can Hear!" *Reader's Digest,* November 1967.
Porter, Sylvia. "Most Common Malady Is Loss of Hearing," *Your Money's Worth,* syndicated, February 2, 1975.

General

"Milk of Kindness Sours, Experts Find," New York *Times,* March 8, 1976.

RECORDINGS

Working in the Sighted World. Vols. I, II, III. New York: American Foundation of the Blind, Recordings, n.d.

Index

Adjustment, defined, 97
Adolescents, 30–31, 70
Adventitious (*See also* specific disabilities); defined, 97
Aesop, 78
African tribe, 92–93
Alexander the Great, 54
Aphasia, 42
Architectural Barriers Act, 88
Aristotle, 46
Armes, Jay J., 78–79
Arthritis, rheumatoid, 75–76
Articles, 103–4
Ataxic cerebral palsy, 57
Athetoid cerebral palsy, 57
Attitudes, 1–19

Bacterial infection, 41
Beethoven, Ludwig van, 6, 48
Beggary, 9, 78
Best Years of Our Lives, The, 78
Bible, 8–9
Bibliography, 99–104
Birth defects. *See* Cripples; specific disabilities
Birth injury. *See* Neurological dysfunctions
Blindisms, 28, 97
Blindness, 6, 8, 14, 18–19, 23, 25–37, 82, 92–93; bibliography on, 99ff., 104
Bone disease, 75
Books, 99–101
Bowley, Agatha H., 59n

Braille, Louis, 31
Braille system, 31; defined, 97
Brain hemorrhage. *See* Strokes
Brain injury (*See also* Neurological dysfunctions): bibliography on, 99, 100, 103–4; and deafness, 42
Brown, Larry, 49
Buddha, and epilepsy, 54
Buddhist monks, 35
Buildings, 88
Byron, George Gordon, Lord, 78

Caesar, Julius, 54
Califano, Joseph, 88
Carlyle, Thomas, 2
Cataracts, 26
Cerebral palsy, 23, 43, 57–62, 68, 81; bibliography on, 101; Deacon case, 81–82
Children, 12–13, 14, 23 (*See also* specific disabilities); infanticide, 8, 13, 77–78
China, blindness in, 35
Christians, 9–10, 46–47
Chronic, defined, 97
Club feet, 75, 78
Cold, common, and deafness, 41
Compensation, defined, 97
Conductive deafness, 41
Congenital (*See also* specific disabilities): defined, 97
Congress, U. S., 87–88

INDEX

Craik, Dinah, 76
Cretinism, 68; Luther and, 10
Cripples, 8–9, 10, 23, 75–79
Crusader, 87n

D'Alonzo, C. A., 64n
Dante Alighieri, and epilepsy, 54
Deacon, Joseph, 81–82
Deaf Adults, 46n
Deafness (hearing defects), 6, 23, 39–50, 82; bibliography on, 99ff., 104; cerebral palsy and, 59, 81
Dentition, abnormal, 43
Deviant, defined, 97
Diabetic retinopathy, 26
Diderot, Denis, 35
Disability/handicap, definitions of, 97–98
Discrimination, defined, 98
Don't Feel Sorry for Paul, 76
Door in the Wall, The, 17
Down's syndrome, 68
Du Bellay, Joachim, 48
Dwarfism, 75; middle ages and, 9, 78

Easter Seal Communicator, 88n
Education, 89–90. *See also* specific disabilities
Egypt, and blindness, 35
Eighteenth century, 10
Employment (jobs; work), 14, 91; and blindness, 33–37; and deafness, 47–50; and epilepsy, 56; and mental retardation, 71; and multiple sclerosis, 65
Encephalitis, 41, 52
Epilepsy, 6, 23, 52–57, 68, 102
Epilepsy: A Teenager's View, 56n
Epilepsy Foundation of America, 56
Epilepsy School Alert, 55n

Facts for Employers About Multiple Sclerosis, 64n

Feet, club, 75, 78
Finger-spelling, 44
"Fool," 71
French, Richard Slayton, 35n
French, and mental retardation, 71
From Homer to Helen Keller, 35n
Frumkin, Robert M., and Frumkin, Miriam Ziesenwine, 29–30, 33

Genetic, defined, 98
German measles, 41, 52
Gesell, Arnold, 45
Glaucoma, 26, 34
Glossary, 97–98
Gore, Thomas, 36
Goret, Morris, 33
Grand mal epilepsy, 53, 55–56
Greece and Greeks, 7, 8, 35, 77–78; and deafness, 46; and epilepsy, 54

Handel, Georg Friedrich, 54
Handicap disability, definitions of, 97–98
Harelip, 43
Hartke, Vance, 49
Havenette, Juan Fernan, 48
Hays, David, 49
Head injury, 52
Health, Education and Welfare, Department of, 88, 89
Hearing aid, 41
Hebraic law, 8–9; and deafness, 46
Hemoplegia, 75
Herodotus, 35
Hesiod, 35
High-tone deafness, 42
Hips, dislocated, 75
Homer, 6, 8, 34
Housing, 92; deafness and, 47
Hydrocephaly, 68
"Hymne à la Surdité," 48

Idiopathic epilepsy, 53
Illiad, the, 6

INDEX

India, blindness in, 35
Infanticide, 8, 13, 77–78
Institutionalization, 10, 13–14. See also specific disabilities
Insurance, epileptics and, 56
Into the Mainstream, 88n

Jesters, court, 9
Jesus Christ, 9
Jobs. See Employment
Jockimo, Paul, 76, 77
Joints, missing, 75
Journal of Rehabilitation, The, 79n
Joyce, Mick, 61–62

Keller, Helen, 39, 82
Kennedy, Joseph P., Jr., F'ndation, 10
Klimet, Stephen A., 88n

Labor, protracted, 52
Larsen, Kathy, 34
Letters on the Blind for the Use of Thou Who See, 35
Leviticus, Book of, 8–9
Lewinson, Edwin R., 19n
Lewis, Joy Schlaben, 79n
Limbs, missing, 75ff., 78–79
Lip-reading, 45ff.
Little Lame Prince, The, 22, 76
Liver, the PKU, 68
Lucretius, 46
Luther, Martin, 9–10, 71

McDonagh, Joe, 36
Macular degeneration, 26
Malnutrition, 68, 52
March, Fredric, 49
Measles, 41, 52
Meningitis, 52
Mental retardation, 9, 23, 67–74, 81, 91, 93; bibliography on, 99, 100, 102–3
Merry Andrews, 9

Middle ages, 9, 71, 78
Miers, Earl Schenck, 84
Milton, John, 34
Mongoloidism, 68
"Monologue of a Deaf Man," 49
Multihandicaps, 81–82
Multiple sclerosis, 52, 62–66, 103
Muscular dystrophy, 52, 66–67, 103
Musical ability, blindness and, 32
Muteness, 42–46

Napoleon, 6, 54
National Theater of the Deaf, 49
Nerve deafness, 41
Nerve disorders. See Neurological dysfunctions
Neurological dysfunctions, 51–74. See also Brain injury; specific disabilities
New Testament, 9
New York Times, 36
Nineteenth century, 10
Ninth Symphony (Beethoven), 48
Nobel, Alfred, 54
Normal, defined, 3–6

Odyssey, the, 6
Old age (aging), 26, 52
Omwake, Eveline B., 29
Orthopedic, defined, 98
Osteomyelitis, 75

Pamphlets and newsletters, 101–3
Paradise Lost, 34
Paul, St., and epilepsy, 54
Percy, Charles, 49
Petit mal epilepsy, 53
Pettingell, Don, 46n
Phenylketonuria, 68
Phineas, 8, 35
Pittakos, 78
PKU, 68
Placental separation, 52
Poisoning, 52
Poling, Daniel A., 62

Polio, 6, 75, 78
Polling, 62, 79n
Poverty, 87
Pregnancy, 41, 52
Prejudice, defined, 98
Premature birth, 52
President's Committee on Employment of the Handicapped, 78
Primitive societies, 7, 13, 92-93
Procrustes legend, 7, 13
Product standards, 88-89
Progressive, defined, 98
Prostheses, 75ff.; defined, 98
Protestant Reformation, 9-10
Psychological and Emotional Aspects of Muscular Dystrophy, 67n
Psychomotor epilepsy, 53

Ramirez, Gilberto, 36
Recordings, 104
Rehabilitation, defined, 98
Rehabilitation Act, 88
Rehabilitation Is . . . , 98
Relapse, defined, 98
Remission, defined, 98
Retardation (*See also* Mental retardation): defined, 98
Retinitis pigmentosa, 26
Reusch, Joseph F., 30n
RH blood, 51-52
Rheumatoid arthritis, 75-76
Rights, handicapped and, 87-93
Rome, ancient, 8, 35, 46
Ronsard, Pierre de, 48
Roosevelt, Franklin D., 6, 78
Russell, Harold, 78

Schmidt, William, 36
Schools, 89-90. *See also* specific disabilities
Shakespeare, William, 78
Sherwin, Albert C., 67n

Shriver, Eunice Kennedy, 73-74, 90
Sign language, 44ff.
Society, defined, 98
Socrates, 54
Solnit, Albert J., 29
Sorrel, Bob, 25, 34
Sparta, 8, 77-78
Spastic cerebral palsy, 57
Special Olympics, 73
Speech and language: blindness and, 27; cerebral palsy and, 59; deafness and, 42-46
Spina bifida, 75
Spinal cord, 52, 75
Spine, curvature of, 75
Sprain, Jane B., 91
Sterilization of epileptics, 56
Strokes, 52, 75
Stuttering, 43
Supreme Court, 90
Symptomatic epilepsy, 53

Tchaikovsky, Peter, 54
Teen-agers. *See* Adolescents
Tempest, The, 78
Tesch, Mary Jane, 79n
Therapy, defined, 98
Thyroid gland, 68
Tiresias, 35
Tongue Tied, 82
Touch, in blind children, 27-28
Treatment, defined, 98
Tumor, brain, 52

United Cerebral Palsy Foundation, 62
Unusual Child, The, 30n

Verbalism, defined, 98
"Village idiot," 71
Villey, Pierre, 37
Viral disease, and deafness, 41
Vision problems (*See also*

Blindness): cerebral palsy and, 81
Volta Review, 45

Wallace, George C., 49
Wolf, Bernard, 76
Work. *See* Employment

World of the Blind, The, 37
Wright, David, 49

X rays, 52

Young Handicapped Child, The, 59n

362.4 Haskins, James
Has   Who are the
        Handicap...

JAME...   ...nior
high ...   the
State ...   ...aten
Island...   ...due
Unive...   ...ida,
Gaine...   ...ook
review...   ...ults
and y...   ...ised
Diary...   ...ook
for D...   ...e of
the m...   ...wn.
James...   and
Magi...   ...on-
violen...   ...lks;
and ...   by
Doub...

HARTFORD PUBLIC LIBRARY

HARTFORD PUBLIC LIBRARY